My Painting Is Done, Now What Do I Do?

Simple Business Systems for Artists
by Suzie Seerey-Lester

The one book every artist should own!

MERMAID PRESS

Copyright ©

Copyright © 2007 by Suzie Seerey-Lester
First Published 2007 in the United States by Mermaid Press LLC
208 Shoreland Drive, Osprey, Florida 34229

Cover & Book Design by John Seerey-Lester © and David Rankin ©
All cartoons by John Seerey-Lester ©

Library of Congress Cataloging in Publication Data
Suzie Seerey-Lester – 1955 –
    My Painting is Done, Now What Do I Do?

All rights reserved. No part of this publication may be reproduced or used in any form or by any means—graphic, electronic, or mechanical, including photocopying, recording, taping, or information storage and retrieval systems—without express written permission of the publisher.

Manufactured and Printed in the USA

First Printing 2007

Disclaimer

This publication is designed to provide general information regarding the business of art. However, laws and practices often vary from state to state and are subject to change. Because each factual situation is different, specific advice should be sought by professionals, such as attorneys, CPAs, and bankers for your precise circumstances. For this reason, the reader is advised to consult with his or her advisors.

The author has taken all reasonable precautions in the preparation of this book and believes the facts presented are accurate at the time of going to press. The author and the publisher do not assume any responsibility for errors or omissions. In addition the author and the publisher specifically disclaim any liability resulting from the use or application of the information contained in this book, and the information is not intended to serve as legal advice related to individual situations.

Dedication

This book is dedicated to John Seerey-Lester, my husband, my best friend, and my mentor. Without his guidance and love, I would still be struggling to discover how to paint. He opens my mind, he opens my eyes, and he opens my heart. What a wonderful adventure he takes me on every day. I am truly a very lucky lady.

Acknowledgements

My thanks goes out to: John Seerey-Lester who taught me everything including many of these systems which he developed and has used for 35 years; Mary Jo Perkins, Jack Perkins, Maureen Snyder, Chuck Snyder, Bob Woelfel, and Jerry Woelfel, better known as "The PhArtists," for all their love, support, and fun Fridays at Studio B while I worked on the book; Sammy & Keith Ulbrick; Bobbie Nash; Linda Thompson; Robert J. Koenke; Herb Booth; Tom Krause; Dale Ludwig; Christine Ludwig for her sharp eyes; and David Rankin. To those artists that offered their wonderful stories: John Banovich, Linda Besse, Pam Brickell, Lee Cable, Brendan Coudal, Kelly Dodge, Joanna Drummond, Tom Hennessey, Matthew Hillier, Denis Leblanc, Dennis Logsdon, Jack Perkins, Julia Rogers, John Sampson, Wes & Rachelle Siegrist, Fran Sweet and Toni Young—we will forever remember these stories, pass them on and make them worse than they really are.

Cartoons by John Seerey-Lester

Winners do what losers won't.

This book is for all the winners out there.

Foreword

The Vital Second Step

Being an artist today just isn't enough in today's competitive marketplace. There are a multitude of amateur and hobby artists, a few successful and those who desire to break into the profitable art market. Where do you go to develop a professional and successful career?

I have found that the artist who has talent and uses good common sensible business and marketing disciplines will succeed. The first step is to produce a fine work of art. The second, and vital step is to become organized and understand the components of the various aspects of the art business. Much of it starts right in your own studio with organization and a **Business and Marketing Plan.** Understanding copyright law, inventory control, recording and cataloging your work, framing, pricing, and getting into the marketplace are aspects that Suzie Seerey-Lester guides you in this important arena of being more than just an artist. It takes business and marketing to get action in selling your work effectively. *My Painting is Done...* provides the assistant that most artists don't have or can't afford. Years of art experience are evident on each page. The experience of Suzie, her husband John Seerey-Lester, and other artists can save readers years of false starts, expensive lessons, and disappointments. Finally a guide to becoming a professional artist that wasn't taught in art school!

While success in the art business takes lots of hard work and selling too, *My Painting is Done...* provides answers and positive direction, with a sprinkling of humor, to the uncertainty and lack of knowledge that many artists have in business and organization. Kudos for this important chronicle that most certainly will help shape many more successful artists in the future.

—**Robert J. Koenke**
Former Publisher, Wildlife Art Magazine
Art Consultant, Educator, Lecturer

Oh, what I would have given...

Having been a professional artist since 1974, I have had some hard times and struggles. As artists, it is tough enough to achieve what we want in our paintings without having the added headache of selling the things. There are many books out there on marketing art, some good and some bad. But before you can market your work, you have to get your ducks (or elephants, depending on what you prefer to paint) in order. We artists are not known for our organizing ability. I am certainly not. I get absorbed in producing a piece and forget everything else. But I have realized over the years there is a lot more to the art business than just painting.

I wish I had a book like this when I started out – oh how wonderful that would have been. I did start a Work Completed Book in a double cash ledger in 1974, and still use it today. I don't know what I would do without it now. So I did do something right. I often look back, with interest, to see what I was being paid for my art in those early days.

When I moved to America and became more successful, I employed a succession of assistants which allowed me to work at the easel instead of doing paper work. Although we have staff now, I learned a lot in those early American years, to "streamline my life" and I can contribute more today towards the running of things because of this.

The important thing I have found, is that the more organized I become in the business end of things, the better my art has become. My mind is clear to create and isn't bogged down with "office stuff."

When I met and married Suzie, I gained not only a life partner, a lover and best buddy, but also a business partner. Her skills amalgamated with mine have given birth to a very diverse and productive studio. We now, not only find time to paint side by side, but also have expanded our organization to successfully market DVD's and Videos, books and organize Master Classes. By bringing our joint resources together and by using better business systems, we have room to expand our business further, and through this wonderful book by Suzie, we can now share this knowledge with other artists.

Unfortunately you don't all have a *Suzie*, but through this book, you do now!

—**John Seerey-Lester**

The author Suzie Seerey-Lester with her husband John
—as always walking on the wild side.

The Author, **Suzie Seerey-Lester**

Who is Suzie Seerey-Lester? Well, besides being married to John Seerey-Lester, one of the World's top wildlife artists, she has been a painter in her own right for many years. But there is more to Suzie than her painting.

For some 30 years she was a diver and diving instructor trainer where she brought her skills to important use when she worked for the CIA teaching CIA agents, Secret Service Agents, FBI and other law enforcement personnel how to dive, as well as other *specialized* skills. Before becoming a professional artist, Suzie worked for several Fortune 500 companies where she excelled in sales and marketing. In her last position at an international corporation she was responsible for more than $2 million in sales per month. She eventually turned to painting full-time, leaving the corporate world behind her, but not forgetting the skills she had acquired along the way. Even so, over the years, she has suffered the pitfalls and hard knocks of selling art that all artists go through. From these experiences, she sharpened her business skills and created these systems to pass on to other artists. When she is not painting, she is in charge of the business end of the Seerey-Lester organization. Suzie now travels all over the globe to paint, from Alaska to Maine, Africa, Guatemala, England and Spain, with her husband John.

Professional Memberships

Suzie is a member of **The Society of Animal Artists** (SAA), **The Wildlife Artists Association** (WAA), **Oil Painters of America** (OPA), **American Society of Marine Artists** (ASMA), **Artists for Conservation** (AFC), and a founding member of **Southern Plein Air Artists** (SPAA) and the **PhArtists**.

Accomplishments & Honors

She has won several distinguished awards for her art including Artist of the Year from the Ocean Foundation, Top 200 and Top 100 in *Arts for the Parks*, and has shown in Bennington Art Museum, Coos Bay Art Museum, Grants Pass Art Museum, and the prestigious Leigh Yawkey Woodson's "Birds in Art". She has sold pieces at Christie's and Sotheby's Art Auctions in London, The National Zoo in Washington, D.C., and the Honolulu Zoo. Suzie was honored by the Raymond James Financial Organization in *Women in Arts* and has had her artwork published in *The Best of Oil Painting* book. Her pieces are collected and shown internationally as well as in several galleries and International Wildlife Shows.

From May until November every year, Suzie volunteers for the Mote Marine Loggerhead Research Program on the "turtle patrol" for the loggerhead turtles.

She is licensed by the State of Florida to identify and verify nests, collect data, rescue and release the endangered baby loggerheads and green turtles.

In 2000 she married world-renowned wildlife artist, John Seerey-Lester. They live, work and play in Florida.

Suzie is considered by many to be a real mermaid.

Contents

My Painting Is Done, Now What Do I Do?
Simple Systems for Artists

Page
- **VII** Foreword: "The Vital Second Step" by Robert J. Koenke
- **VIII** "Oh, What I would have given…" by John Seerey-Lester
- **IX** The Author, Suzie Seerey-Lester

Chapter 1 — How do I keep track of my paintings? *Starts Page 15*

Page
- **15** Original Log Sheet
- **17** Work Completed Book
- **20** Labeling the Painting
- **21** Copyright Label
- **22** Notice Label
- **23** Review

Chapter 2 — What on earth happened to that painting? *Page 25*

Page
- **25** Inventory of Originals
- **26** Sold Inventory List
- **27** Where Have they Been List
- **28** Review

Chapter 3 — Photographing the work *Starts Page 29*

Page
- **29** Using a Professional Photographer
- **30** Do It Yourself
- **32** Bad Photographs
- **38** Good Photographs
- **39** Photo Prints
- **39** Digital Prints
- **39** Slides
- **41** Filing Slides
- **42** Follow the Directions
- **44** Review

Chapter 4 — Framing the artwork — Starts Page 45

Page
- 45 Varnishing Acrylic Paintings
- 45 Varnishing Oil Paintings
- 46 Ready to Frame
- 46 Using a Point Driver Gun
- 47 Using Mirror Clips
- 50 Framing
- 51 Framing Costs
- 51 Customizing Frames
- 52 Ordering Frames Ahead of Time
- 52 Framing under glass
- 53 Papering the back of the frame
- 60 Review

Chapter 5 — The business side of things — Starts Page 61

Page
- 61 Starting a Procedure Manual
- 62 Copyrighting
- 64 Licensing Your Work
- 65 Creating a Business Name and License
- 66 Creating a Logo
- 66 Creating your Biography
- 67 Designing a Website
- 68 Accepting Commissions
- 69 Keeping a Scrapbook
- 70 Keeping a Photo Album
- 70 Using Software
- 71 Writing a Painting Paragraph
- 72 VIP Program
- 73 Newsletter
- 74 Open Studio Sale
- 76 Review

Chapter 6 — Consigning your artwork — Starts Page 77

Page
- 77 Consignment Agreement
- 79 Dealing Direct with Clients
- 82 Review

Chapter 7 — **Setting your price** Starts Page 83

Page
- 84 Finding a Mentor
- 85 Setting the Price
- 85 By the Inch
- 86 Framing Costs
- 86 Recommending a Retail Price
- 88 Review

Chapter 8 — **Off to the market** Starts Page 89

Page
- 89 Shipping and Handling
- 89 Shipping to a Client
- 96 Shipping to the Event
- 97 Packaging
- 97 Crates
- 98 Specialized Boxes
- 100 Actual Shipping
- 100 International Shipping
- 102 Review

Chapter 9 — **The exhibition** Starts Page 103

Page
- 103 Show Inventory List
- 104 Box System
- 105 Booth Plan
- 106 Setting up the Booth
- 110 Getting Psyched for a Show
- 110 Red Dots
- 111 Not for Profit Shows
- 111 Other Types of Shows
- 113 Building a Relationship with your clients
- 114 Assembling your own Booth (Tents)
- 118 Photo Book
- 118 Price Cards
- 118 Price Tags
- 119 Writing a Painting Paragraph
- 120 Leaving the booth

120 Sales
123 Show Check List
126 Show Breakdown
126 Auctions
124 Not For Profit Shows
124 Other Types of Shows
128 Review

Chapter 10 — Artist etiquette Starts page 129

Page
129 Don't Burn your Bridges
129 Visit Shows, All Kinds
130 Don't Bring your Portfolio to another Artist's Space
133 Follow the Show Rules
134 Don't Photograph other's Artwork
134 Workshop Etiquette
136 Review

Chapter 11 — Defending yourself against stupidity or A funny thing happened to me on the way to the show Starts page 137

Page
137 True Stories from Shows

Chapter 12 — Recommended resources list Starts Page 151

Page
155 Image Index
157 Key Points Index

Chapter 1

How do I keep track of my paintings?

You have worked hard creating just the right image. You have researched, sketched it out, and erased it numerous times, until you are happy with the composition. The time spent actually painting could take days, weeks, or months until you are finally pleased with the results. But what do you do after you put the paintbrush down?

Original Information Sheet

Let's create an *Original Information Sheet*. This sheet will help you keep track of the painting during several stages until you are ready to ship it out. You start this sheet when you begin the painting. It will be a quick reference for everything about the painting. After you have taken a photograph (See Chapter 3) of the painting, attach it to the sheet. After it has sold, you can update the sheet with the purchaser's name and price. Keep these sheets in a separate three ring binder (use different color binders for different subjects).

This is what the sheet will contain:

- **Date:** When you actually started the painting
- **Title**
- **Size**
- **Medium**
- **Value**
- **Purpose** –
  Is it for a specific show?
  Going to a special gallery?
- **Signed**
- **WC# created**
- **Title Label**
- **© Copyright Label**
- **Varnished**
- **Framed**
- **Nameplate**
- **Licensing Potential**
- **Photographed**
  Photo print made
  Transparencies made
  Slides being made
  Attach photo to this sheet

Bright Idea Studio
1221 South Adams
Osprey, Fl 34229

(222) 222-2222
brightideastudio@aol.com
www.BrightIdeaStudio.com

Original Information Sheet

Date Started: _____

Title of Painting: _____

Size: _____ Medium: _____

Retail Price: _____

Purpose of the Painting _____
_____

Check ✓ when completed:

- Signed by artist ☐
- Label on Painting ☐
- Photographed ☐
- Varnished ☐
- Licensing Potential ☐
- Photo Attached ☐
- WC# Created ☐
- Copyright © ☐
- Slides Taken ☐
- Framed ☐
- Name Plate ☐

Work Completed Book

Your next step is a *Work Completed Book* (WC book), which will become your permanent record of all your paintings. You should keep a record from the first painting you created to the one you just finished. How? What does it look like?

If you are not computer literate (or do not have a spouse who is keeping your records) you can manually log your *WC Book* (using crayons, pencil, pen, or even rocks). Go to Office Depot, Office Max, Staples or just your local stationery store and purchase an accounting book. You need a book with 8 columns to collect all your data, preferably ring bound.

If you have a computer and know how to turn it on, you can use an excel spreadsheet to record all your WC info. (Excel is easy to use, easy to install, and easy to find). Once we type in the data, we can then retrieve it by the date, the title, or the subject, and print it out for easy reference. The columns that you will need (and feel free to add any additional ones to suit your needs) are:

WC# — You will assign a number to each piece, as your *WC Number*. One way you can start is with the year the painting was painted, and the number of paintings you have done. For example: The first painting you complete in the year 2007 would be listed as: 07/01. That way, by a quick glance you can tell the year you painted the piece, and it will be easier to locate later. Another method could be to start at *Painting 001*, which will now be known as WC# 001. If you are doing this by hand in the accounting book, you could use, for example, the page number, then the line number on that page, i.e. Page 1 line 6 would read as WC# 1/6. You need to choose the method that suits your needs best, or is the easiest to set up and remember how to use.

Date: — This is the date you completed the painting. You do not have to use the exact date; you may want to use only the month and year to make it easy.

Title: — Give each piece a name! You can use the subject in the title as well in parentheses (), or followed by a dash, for example: *Evening Sojourn - Ibis, Great White Hunter (Great White Egret), Reflections in Nature.*

Subject: — What is the painting about? Ibis, Landscape, Still Life with Oranges, Portrait.

Size: Enter the height of the piece first, for example a 9 x 12 is a horizontal, 12 x 9 is a vertical.
Medium: Oil, Acrylic, Watercolor, Pastel, Graphite, etc.
Wholesale: What do you want to receive for this painting?

Usually the wholesale price is 60% of the retail value. For example, your retail price for your 9 x 12 painting is $1000.00; the wholesale price is $600.00. Each gallery or show may have a different *commission* structure, so you will change your wholesale price accordingly. For example, Gallery A is working on the 60-40 percentage, (you receive 60%); Gallery B is working on a 50-50 structure. This must be reflected in the paperwork.

Retail: What is the retail price? This is the price that the painting sells for, in a Gallery, show or on the Internet.
Comments: Any special comments you want to make. Have you painted it for a specific show or event? Or leave it blank and put the buyer's name in when it has sold.

Here is an actual spreadsheet that you can use for your WC book.

Your Name Here - Original Work Completed Book

WC#	Date	Title	Subject	Size	Medium	Wholesale	Retail
06/49	12/1/06	Great White Hunter	White Egret	8x10	Oil	$ 480.00	$ 800.00
06/50	12/7/06	Evening Dash - Jaguar	Jaguar	9x12	Acrylic	$ 900.00	$ 1,500.00
06/51	12/15/06	Early Risers	Doves & Barn	9x12	Acrylic	$ 900.00	$ 1,500.00
07/01	1/5/07	Reflections of Nature	Spoonbills	12x24	Acrylic	$ 2,100.00	$ 3,500.00
07/02	1/25/07	Morning Stroll	Wood Stork	8x16	Oil	$ 1,800.00	$ 3,000.00
07/03	1/30/07	Morning Preen	Ibis	12x9	Acrylic	$ 900.00	$ 1,500.00
07/04	2/2/07	Low Tide	Willits	11x14	Acrylic	$ 660.00	$ 1,100.00
07/05	2/12/07	Southern Nights	Penguins	8x10	Acrylic	$ 480.00	$ 800.00
07/06	3/1/07	Sitting on a Sandbar	White Pelican	8x16	Oil	$ 1,800.00	$ 3,000.00
07/07	3/21/07	Silent Stalker	Great Blue Heron	12x24	Oil	$ 2,100.00	$ 3,500.00
07/08	4/25/07	Dark Reflections	Swan	9x12	Oil	$ 600.00	$ 1,000.00
07/09	5/5/07	One Flew Over the Cupola	Sand Hill Cranes	12x24	Acrylic	$ 2,100.00	$ 3,500.00
07/10	5/15/07	Evening Sojourn	Ibis	15x30	Oil	$ 2,400.00	$ 4,000.00
07/11	6/6/07	Vanishing Point	Spoonbills	12x24	Acrylic	$ 2,100.00	$ 3,500.00

When referring to the WC#, you could use the system above, or simply number starting at 1, or 100, or your own system.

Keep a copy of your *WC Book* on a CD as a back up, and on your hard drive. Start a three ring binder called *WC Book*, have two paper copies; one chronological, starting with your last painting and ending with your first painting. The other copy should be alphabetized by title. That way you have a quick reference if you are looking up *Reflections in Nature* and can't remember what the WC# is or when you completed the painting. Using a spread sheet is a wonderful tool, if you log all the subjects. You could even alphabetize by the subject if you needed to look up all the paintings you have done on Cheetahs, or Lions, etc.

Note: *The WC#* you have created will be shown on everything related to the painting, i.e. labels on photographs, slides, and transparencies, invoices, certificates of original artwork, prints and licensing. This will be covered later.

Your Name - Work Completed Book - by Alpha

WC#	Date	Title	Subject	Size	Medium	Wholesale	Retail
07/08	4/25/07	Dark Reflections	Swan	9x12	Oil	$ 900.00	$ 1,500.00
06/51	12/15/06	Early Risers	Doves & Barn	9x12	Acrylic	$ 900.00	$ 1,500.00
06/50	12/7/06	Evening Dash - Jaguar	Jaguar	9x12	Acrylic	$ 900.00	$ 1,500.00
07/10	5/15/07	Evening Sojourn	Ibis	15x30	Oil	$ 2,400.00	$ 4,000.00
06/49	12/1/06	Great White Hunter	White Egret	8x10	Oil	$ 480.00	$ 800.00
07/04	2/2/07	Low Tide	Willits	11x14	Acrylic	$ 1,200.00	$ 2,000.00
07/03	1/30/07	Morning Preen	Ibis	12x9	Acrylic	$ 900.00	$ 1,500.00
07/02	1/25/07	Morning Stroll	Wood Stork	8x16	Oil	$ 1,800.00	$ 3,000.00
07/09	5/5/07	One Flew Over the Cupola	Sand Hill Cranes	12x24	Acrylic	$ 2,100.00	$ 3,500.00
07/01	1/5/07	Reflections of Nature	Spoonbills	12x24	Acrylic	$ 2,100.00	$ 3,500.00
07/07	3/21/07	Silent Stalker	Great Blue Heron	12x24	Oil	$ 2,100.00	$ 3,500.00
07/06	3/1/07	Sitting on a Sandbar	White Pelican	8x16	Oil	$ 1,800.00	$ 3,000.00
07/05	2/12/07	Southern Nights	Penguins	8x10	Acrylic	$ 480.00	$ 800.00
07/11	6/6/07	Vanishing Point	Spoonbills	12x24	Acrylic	$ 2,100.00	$ 3,500.00

When referring to the WC#, you could use the system above, or simply number starting at 1, or 100, or your own system.

Label the Painting

Now that you have finished logging on the *Original Information Sheet*, and the *WC Book*, the next step is easy. On the back of every painting place a label with:

Title (*bold and larger print than the rest of the label*)
Your Name _____
WC# _____
Size and Medium _____

You want this label on the back of every piece that goes out. If you are shipping several paintings to one location, the recipient can now tell the difference between *Great White Hunter – (Great White Egret)* and *Reflections in Nature*. Also, even though you have signed the painting, a gallery or show can easily identify your piece from everyone else's, because your name is clearly recorded on the back. We recommend standard *Avery Address Labels #8163*.

Reflections of Nature By Suzie Seerey-Lester WC# 07/01 12x24 Acrylic on Linen	**Title** By Your Name WC# Size, Medium
Title By Your Name WC# Size, Medium	**Title** By Your Name WC# Size, Medium
Title By Your Name WC# Size, Medium	**Title** By Your Name WC# Size, Medium
Title By Your Name WC# Size, Medium	**Title** By Your Name WC# Size, Medium

While you are creating the single label for the back of the painting, run a ½ sheet of the smaller labels (8160) to put on the back of the photographs of the painting. We will discuss this later.

Copyright label

The next label that should be placed on the back of your painting is the copyright label. This should protect you from copyright infringements, or at least inform people that you retain the copyright, and they need to seek your permission to use it in any form. We generally run off several sheets of these labels so they are handy when we need them. Again we use the *Avery 8163* labels. It should read:

The artist reserves all reproduction rights, including the right to claim statutory copyright in the work. The work may not be photographed, sketched, painted, or reproduced in any manner whatsoever, without the express, written consent of the artist. All approved reproductions shall bare the following copyright notice by **Your Name Here** ©.

Notice Label

The final label that should be placed on the back of the painting is a *notice* label, to let people know that the artwork is undamaged when they receive it. Label 8164 works the best. It should read:

Notice

This is original, damage-free artwork. Any damage sustained while in your possession must be repaired at your expense.

In the event such damage is non-repairable or if this artwork is lost while in your custody, care, or control, you are liable for all costs and/or damages sustained by the owner as the result of such damage or loss.

NOTICE	NOTICE
This is original, damage-free artwork. Any Damage sustained while in your possession Must be repaired at your expense. In the event such damage is un-repairable Or if this artwork is lost while in your custody, Care, or control, you are liable for all Costs and/or damages sustained by the Owner as the result of such damage or loss.	This is original, damage-free artwork. Any Damage sustained while in your possession Must be repaired at your expense. In the event such damage is un-repairable Or if this artwork is lost while in your custody, Care, or control, you are liable for all Costs and/or damages sustained by the Owner as the result of such damage or loss.
NOTICE	**NOTICE**
This is original, damage-free artwork. Any Damage sustained while in your possession Must be repaired at your expense. In the event such damage is un-repairable Or if this artwork is lost while in your custody, Care, or control, you are liable for all Costs and/or damages sustained by the Owner as the result of such damage or loss.	This is original, damage-free artwork. Any Damage sustained while in your possession Must be repaired at your expense. In the event such damage is un-repairable Or if this artwork is lost while in your custody, Care, or control, you are liable for all Costs and/or damages sustained by the Owner as the result of such damage or loss.
NOTICE	**NOTICE**
This is original, damage-free artwork. Any Damage sustained while in your possession Must be repaired at your expense. In the event such damage is un-repairable Or if this artwork is lost while in your custody, Care, or control, you are liable for all Costs and/or damages sustained by the Owner as the result of such damage or loss.	This is original, damage-free artwork. Any Damage sustained while in your possession Must be repaired at your expense. In the event such damage is un-repairable Or if this artwork is lost while in your custody, Care, or control, you are liable for all Costs and/or damages sustained by the Owner as the result of such damage or loss.

Using your *Original Information Sheet*, start to check off the list as you complete tasks associated with the painting. When the painting is ready to be shipped off, you want to make sure that anyone who opens the box, knows that this is your painting. We call it *"making it idiot proof."* The easier you make your painting identifiable and ready for the gallery or show, the more ready the gallery or show will be to accept your pieces.

Review:

- **Create an *Original Information Sheet*:**

    Date Completed
    Title
    Size
    Medium
    Retail Price
    Purpose
    Photographed
    Signed
    WC# Created
    Label on the back of painting
    Copyright Label on back of painting
    Varnished
    Framed
    Name Plate
    Transparency
    Slides
    Attach a photograph of painting to sheet

- **Create a W-C Book with the following Information:**

  WC#
  Date
  Title
  Subject
  Size
  Medium
  Wholesale Price
  Retail Price
  Comments

- **Make sheets of labels:**

  Painting Label
  Labels for the Back of Photographs
  Copyright Labels
  Notice Labels

Chapter 2

What on earth happened to that painting?

The Dreaded Inventory

How do you keep track of all the paintings you create? Where are they? Where have they been? What is the value? Even more important, what is your percentage of sale price? All of these are aspects of the business side of painting that we all hate to do. So make it easy. Let the computer do all the work for you. Yes, another three ring binder and another spreadsheet!

Inventory of Originals

The purpose of this spread sheet is to keep track of your inventory as you create the paintings and ship to different galleries and shows. This sheet will constantly change as you make more paintings, move them around and sell them. You will want to keep a back up on a disc or CD and on your hard drive as well as the all important paper copy. Put your inventory in a different colored binder from the *WC Book*, so you can easily pick it out by the color of the binder. In this binder you will track inventory with the *Inventory of Originals, Sold Originals* and *Where Have They Been?* lists.

Start your spreadsheet with a column for the WC number, the second column with the Title, then columns for Size, Medium, Wholesale, Retail, Date, Gallery, Date, Gallery, Date Gallery. The width of the columns will depend upon the information to be documented. Now add the information for each painting in the *"rows."* The last few columns are to be used when a painting is moved from one location to another before selling it. If a painting is moved more than 4 times, then it will be added to the *Where Have They Been* list, for better tracking. Lay out this spread sheet in a landscape format so you can get more columns on the sheet. See the attached example of the *Inventory of Originals*.

Here is an example of an *Inventory of Originals List:*

Inventory of Original Paintings — 7/7/07

WC#	Title	Size	Medium	Wholesale	Retail	Date	Gallery
07/08	Dark Reflections	9x12	Oil	$ 600.00	$ 1,000.00	Jun-07	O Gallery
06/51	Early Risers - Dove & Barn	9x12	Acrylic	$ 900.00	$ 1,500.00	Dec-07	ABC
07/10	Evening Sojourn	15x30	Oil	$ 2,400.00	$ 4,000.00	Jul-07	Q Gallery
06/49	Great White Hunter	8x10	Oil	$ 480.00	$ 800.00	Dec-07	M Gallery
07/04	Low Tide - Willits	11x14	Oil	$ 660.00	$ 1,100.00	Feb-07	HI Gallery
07/03	Morning Preen - Ibis	9x12	Acrylic	$ 900.00	$ 1,500.00	Oct-07	M Gallery
07/02	Morning Stroll - Wood Stork	8x16	Oil	$ 1,800.00	$ 3,000.00	Sep-07	HI Gallery
07/09	One Flew Over The Cupola	12x24	Acrylic	$ 2,100.00	$ 3,500.00	Jun-07	P Gallery
07/01	Reflections of Nature	12x24	Acrylic	$ 2,100.00	$ 3,500.00	May-07	Q Gallery
07/06	Sitting on a Sandbar	8x16	Oil	$ 1,800.00	$ 3,000.00	Apr-07	M Gallery
07/05	Southern Nights	8x10	Acrylic	$ 480.00	$ 800.00	Mar-07	ABC
07/11	Vanishing Point	12x24	Acrylic	$ 2,100.00	$ 3,500.00	Jul-07	HI Gallery

Note: We suggest that you keepo this list in alphabetical order

Note: We suggest that you keep this list in alphabetical order.

It is easy to keep an alphabetized list for fast reference. Note that on the example, the date is placed in the upper right corner of the sheet. Every time you update the list, update the date as well, and then you can quickly see when you last worked on your sheet.

Sold Inventory

Once the painting has sold remove it from the *Inventory of Originals List* and add it to the *Sold Inventory List*. This way you can keep track of what has been sold, to whom it has been sold and the price. This is also a lot of fun to look through after several years so you can see how your prices have increased, who has been purchasing them, and where they sell the best. You can use this information to market yourself better in the future. If you know that you are selling more pieces in galleries, than for example booth shows, from the data on the *Sold Inventory List*, market towards galleries more and shows less. This is also the start of collecting information on who is purchasing your originals. You want to keep good records on clients, for further marketing.

The simplest way to create the *Sold Inventory List* is a new spreadsheet. The *Sold Inventory List* will have most of the information that your inventory sheet will have. As always, start with the WC#, Title, Size, Medium and Retail Price. One column should be headed *Sold To,* and any additional information important to you such as the event, i.e. where it sold i.e., at Quail Unlimited, World Wildlife Fund, should be included. This is fun to look back on years later and see who has your paintings, and the prices they originally sold for.

Sold Inventory Sheet 7/7/07

WC#	Title	Size	Medium	Subject	Retail	Date	Sold To:
6/15	A Time to Remember	12x24	Acrylic	Barn Owl	$ 3,500.00	Jul-07	Susan Ryan
06/02	Birds of a Feather	9x12	Acrylic	Doves	$ 1,500.00	Dec-06	Jonathan Brown
05/23	Dark Passages	9x12	Oil	Swan	$ 1,000.00	Jun-07	Mr. James Smith
05/14	Family Affair	11x14	Oil	Dolphins	$ 1,100.00	Feb-07	Robyn O'N eil
03/34	Film at Nine	8x10	Oil	Crows	$ 800.00	Jan-07	Rose Walters
05/18	Fly By	12x24	Acrylic	Sand Hill Cranes	$ 3,500.00	Nov-07	P Gallery
06/11	Maui Morning	9x12	Acrylic	Humpback Whales	$ 1,500.00	Oct-07	Christies Auction
04/7	Mountain Moonlight	8x16	Oil	Landscape	$ 3,000.00	Apr-07	M Gallery
05/30	Once Upon A Time	8x10	Acrylic	Loggerhead Turtles	$ 800.00	Mar-07	James Guilira
06/02	Spoonbill Reflections	12x24	Acrylic	Spoonbills	$ 3,500.00	May-07	Q Gallery
04/3	The Meeting Place	8x16	Oil	Old Barn	$ 3,000.00	Sep-07	David Sheppard Fund
04/19	Two Coy	15x30	Oil	Coy Fish	$ 4,000.00	Jul-07	Shirley Pendit

Note: We suggest that you keepo this list in alphabetical order

Note: We suggest that you keep this in alphabetical order.

Where Have They Been?

When you start moving paintings to different galleries and shows, make sure that the same piece does not go back to the same venue or event that it just came from. You can start on the *Original Information Sheet*, with the first three or four moves; anything over four moves will be added to the *Where Have They Been* list. Again using a spreadsheet you just need the WC number, title, then the dates and galleries/shows where the individual piece has visited, or sold. Every time you move a piece, update your *Where Have They Been* list.

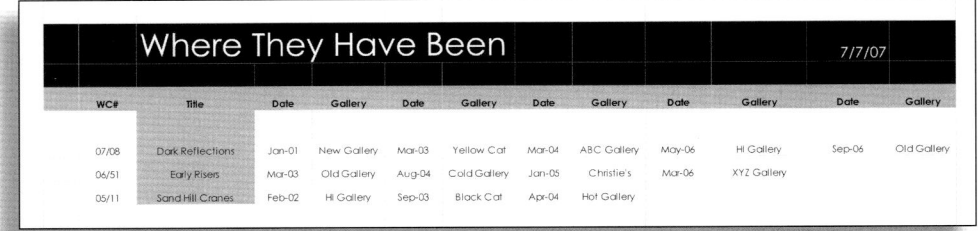

We suggest that you create this form in the landscape format to be able to have more galleries and dates to be logged on one page.

Review:

- Create an *Inventory of Originals,* listing all inventory
- Create a *Sold Inventory Sheet* listing all sold paintings
- Create a *Where Have They Been Sheet* listing placement history

Chapter 3

Photographing your work

First Impressions are Lasting

When you show a gallery or client your work, you want to impress them. The best way of doing this is to ensure that the painting is photographed properly. The best place to start is with a professional photographer in your area. Have them photograph the paintings on a black background. Depending on what you want to do with the work, select 35 mm slides, transparencies, or digital shots to be taken. Don't have heart failure! Professional photographers are not that expensive. You need to ask yourself, are you worth the best photographs? Do you want to get your artwork into galleries, shows or publishers? Do you want to be a professional artist, or a Sunday painter? This is the first image a prospect will see of your work, and while a good photo could get you accepted, a bad one will hurt your chances. Think about it, if you send a gallery poorly taken slides of your work, the next time you submit, they may not even review them. Give yourself the best opportunity to get a foot-in-the-door.

Using a Professional Photographer

A professional photographer will make your painting look great in any format. Interview different photographers to find out their specialty. Be sure to discuss your needs with the photographer. Explain to them for what purpose the images will be used. They may have suggestions on how to get the best quality, for the best price. Ask them to photograph the paintings with a color bar/gray scale.

Always discuss the price prior to giving them your work to shoot. Do they charge by the hour, or by the image? Most photographers will have a printed price sheet that you can keep. Now you can determine if you want to order 20 slides, or only 12. Digital scans are also important to have produced on a CD. You can make a copy of the CD and send it to clients or galleries. Currently, most shows and competitions require slides to view the work. When it comes to printing your image in a catalog or book, they may accept a digital image or require a transparency. We suggest that you have at least 12 slides and one digital CD created. From the CD you can make prints to send out.

It is probably a good idea to have the photographer do a test shoot. It is important that the photographer undertakes color correction on your behalf. This will usually cost extra, but it is worth it. The photographic image should match as closely as possible to the original painting, otherwise it is useless.

You are hiring the photographer to photograph your work. You own the negatives, and you own all the rights to the images. A good photographer will sign a simple letter from you stating that you own the copyright.

The letter should include the following information:

Today's Date

_____ (your name) is hiring _____ (the photographer's name and company) to photograph my artwork. Since this is a work-for-hire arrangement, it is understood that I own the photographic digital card or negatives taken of my artwork and that those digital cards or negatives shall be given to me, and no one else. The artist reserves all reproduction rights including the right to claim statutory copyright in the work being photographed. The work may not be sketched, painted, or reproduced in any manner whatsoever without the express written consent of the artist. All approved reproductions shall bare the following copyright notice by © your name.

Do It Yourself

Ok, ok, the professional photographer is 2 hours away, and you need to send slides out by the end of the week. Your best friend is a great photographer, and wants to help you out. Be careful, if the photographs are not the highest quality, that's how your work will be considered.

When a judge or gallery owner views your slides, they may only concentrate on it for 3 seconds, so you need to capture their attention quickly. You want them to see your entire piece in as much detail as possible in one shot. **Remember you have 3 seconds**. You need to have the shot focused, with no distractions around the painting. Be sure to sign and use the copyright symbol before you photograph.

Take the painting out of the frame before it is photographed. The frame may dominate the painting; create a cast shadow; be too dark for the painting and prevent reflected light from hitting the surface of the painting. Or it may not suit the recipient's taste so it could have an adverse effect. Since it will distract from the painting, take it out of the frame before you photograph.

Obtain a *"gray card or gray scale"* from a local photography supply store, and place it over the lower right or left corner of the painting. The first shot should include this, and then remove it for the remainder of shots. This will be a necessary guide for the person processing the film or digital image. Make sure you tell the photo processor what you are doing so they too can monitor the images correctly.

Varnish the painting **after** it is photographed. The varnish may reflect the light and cause specks (speculars) of light on the photograph.

Start with a black wall outside in the shade. Your landlord won't let you paint the wall black? Cover the wall with a black cloth. Another suggestion is to wrap a black cloth around a Styrofoam board. This is lightweight and can be moved easily. Or attach a black cloth to a bar and hang it over the easel. Or paint a piece of Masonite flat black to put on your easel, making sure it is larger than the painting to be photographed. Find what will work for you. The objective is to have a flat black background surrounding your painting when it is photographed. Focus in so that the painting fills the screen, as much as the proportions of the piece allow. Make sure the painting is not cropped. It is okay to see the black background around the painting, but nothing else. After all, you want everyone to see all of the painting! Place the camera on a tripod, so it is nice and steady, a focused shot, and the painting and camera are parallaxed. To achieve this the camera has to be square with the image being photographed. If the painting is slightly angled on the easel, then the camera on the tripod should be at the same angle. This will eliminate any distortion. Use a telephoto or zoom lens and focus in on the entire painting. You want to make sure the aperture is as open as possible, i.e., 1.8, and the shutter speed is as fast as the light allows.

By following these suggestions you should get the best results. The painting will not get noticed if you see the back fence with the shovel and trash cans, or your painting so small they can't see what the subject is, or if Rover the dog got in the way or is casting a shadow. Or the painting is at such an angle so as to cause distortion. A common error is caused by light from behind the camera (even when shooting in the shade) that causes a shine on one part of the painting. Take your time and make sure it's picture perfect before you press the shutter. A cable release is also recommended, to prevent camera shake.

If shooting digitally, store the photographs on a hard drive using the *WC #* you have created for the painting. Also make a copy on a CD, again storing them by their *WC#*. Make two contact sheets, one for the CD, and the second in a three ring binder marked CD contact sheets. Label each CD with a number, and the same number should correspond to the contact sheet. CD #1, will also be Contact Sheet #1. Now you can easily look up a specific image on any CD. There are also several software programs that will make your life easier; these are worth checking out.

Here are some examples of bad photos: These might seem extreme, but it really does happen.

You can't see the painting for the shadow and all the "stuff" which is very distracting.

When a judge or a gallery owner sees a photo like this, you may be disqualified, because there are too many distractions.

First impressions count. Make the most of it, do not include your yard ornaments.

If you shoot the painting at an extreme angle, you are losing the full impact of the image.

Another example of an extreme angle, not recommended, especially with the tire in the background. It screams "amateur."

You want to keep it parallel to the edge of the photo, not at an angle.

When photographing make sure that you don't use a flash which will bounce off your painting. It distorts and obscures the image.

The one thing you should never ever do is photograph the painting next to a "port-a-potty." These examples may be extreme, but believe it or not, we have seen all of these examples when judging shows and critiquing in class.

It is imperative that your image is in complete focus. If the recipient can't identify what it is, you will not impress anyone.

Hands and fingers do not make great accents to your painting. Again it is distracting.

Lovely garden?? Can't see the painting well because of all the stuff and the cast shadow.

The proper way to photograph; black or neutral background, using a tripod, making sure it is parallaxed, and has no distracting backgrounds.

This is the proper way to have your work photographed. You see the full image without frame or other distractions.

Photographic Prints

Now you are beginning to set up systems for prints of the photographs of your paintings. Have at least 12 (4x6") prints of each of the paintings. Ok, so now you have all these prints. So what do you do with them? First of all, label them.

You have already made sheets of labels, one containing the label for the back of the painting and the remainder of the labels for the back of the photos. (See Chapter 1). If you send the print out, it needs to have all the information, clearly typed in a professional manner on the back of the photograph. Then file the remaining labeled photos by *WC#* in a photo box (or other appropriate storage system). Yes, believe it or not, some galleries and clients still want to see photos. You may also need to send them to magazines, newspapers, or to accompany news about yourself.

Digital

If you are digitally photographing your paintings, do it at the highest possible resolution. Then store them on the computer by *WC#*. After you have completed several digital photographs (of several different paintings) burn them on a CD with a thumbnail of all the photos, by *WC#* so they are easy to find and print. Remember, store them on a hard drive, on a CD/DVD and have a paper copy. When needed, a print can be produced, labeled and sent out as discussed earlier. Some galleries, museums, shows, etc., are now accepting digital photographs. Be sure to follow their specific instructions when sending it to them. If they ask for 75 dpi, do not send 300. Follow their instructions, and if you are not sure, call the gallery or recipient and find out what they would prefer. Do not burn your bridges with a gallery before you even get started.

A new eager artist sent his entire portfolio (unsolicited) via e-mail. When the gallery owner arrived in the morning and started answering e-mails, the artist's file was so large that it tied up the computer for half the day. The gallery owner was extremely upset. This artist destroyed any opportunity he may have had, for years to come, to be reviewed by this gallery, and I am sure any gallery in the same area—a missed opportunity to make a good first impression.

Slides

You should take at least 12 slides of each piece. It is better to have more taken to begin with so you don't have to make dupes of the last slide, which will reduce the quality and color. If you have taken the slides yourself, and you did not use the black background, you will need to strip the slides.

To strip slides it will be necessary to purchase special silver photographic tape. This unique tape is designed not to burn or catch on fire when viewed in a slide projector. You don't want to start that sort of fire with your slide when trying to get into a show. Place the silver tape on the slide over the area surrounding the painting. When the slide is viewed the silver tape becomes black and only the painting is displayed. This is special tape designed for this purpose; don't use substitute tape.

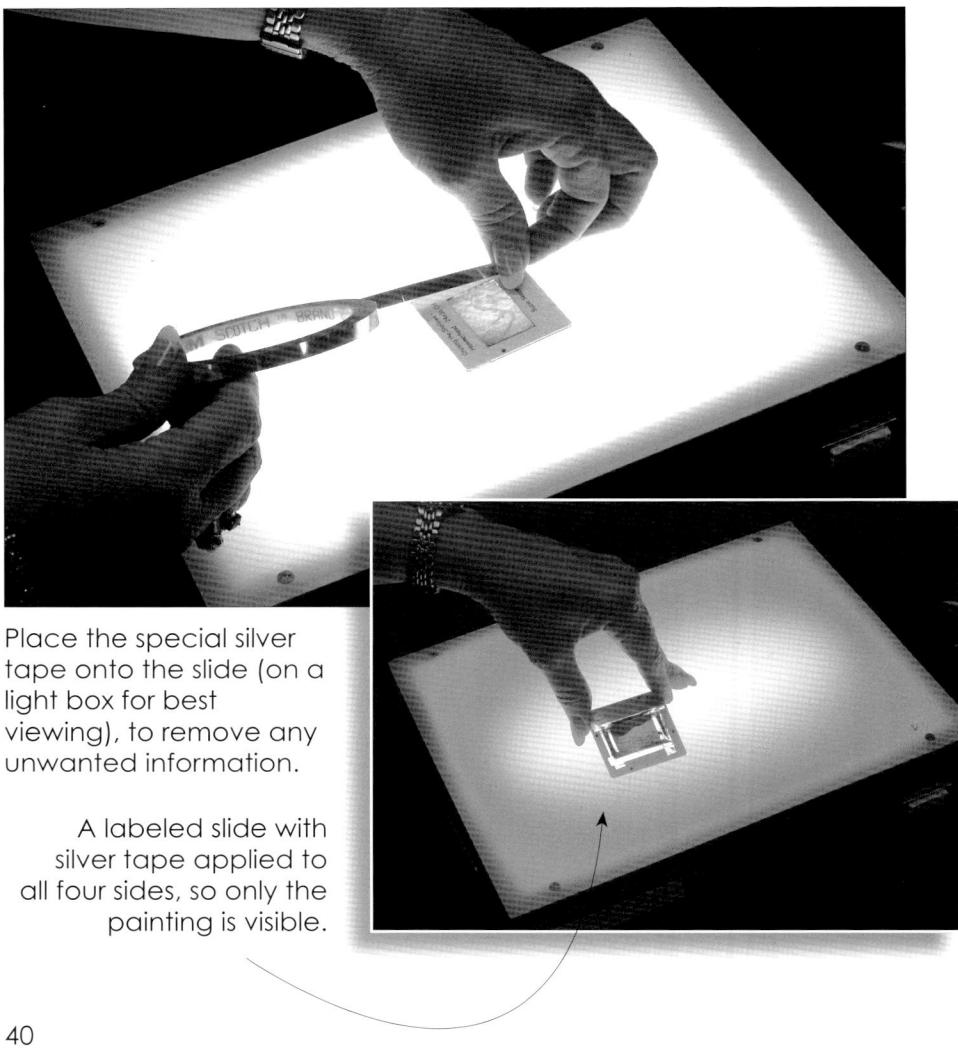

Place the special silver tape onto the slide (on a light box for best viewing), to remove any unwanted information.

A labeled slide with silver tape applied to all four sides, so only the painting is visible.

Filing Slides

When you get your 35 mm slides, put them in sleeves and into a three ring binder. Do not label them until you are ready to send them out. Each show or gallery may require a specific way of labeling the slide. If you pre label the slide it may not comply with their requirements, and it may be rejected immediately. In the three ring binder you can sort them by *WC#*, Title, Medium, (Oil, Acrylic, etc.) Subject i.e. Primates, Bears, Big Cats, Plein Air, Landscapes, Figurative, etc. Set up a system that makes it easy for you to find the slides quickly.

Three ring binder to store your sheets of slides.

Sheets of your slides sorted by WC#, or subject, or medium etc., what ever helps you find them.

Follow the Directions

When you are submitting to a show, FOLLOW THE DIRECTIONS. If they ask for your name at the bottom, and the title at the top, be sure to label it that way. The fastest way to be rejected from a show or gallery is not to follow the directions. If the judge can see the slide is not marked properly, they may not view it. If you can't follow simple instructions on labeling a slide, you won't be able to follow directions to be in a show, and the organizers will probably not select you. There are special labels designed just for slides: (**Slide Pro Labels** Catalog # LL-SR and are available from: Image Innovations, Inc. 1-800-345-4118.) Keep a careful log of where slides and trannies have been sent so you can make sure they are returned when required.

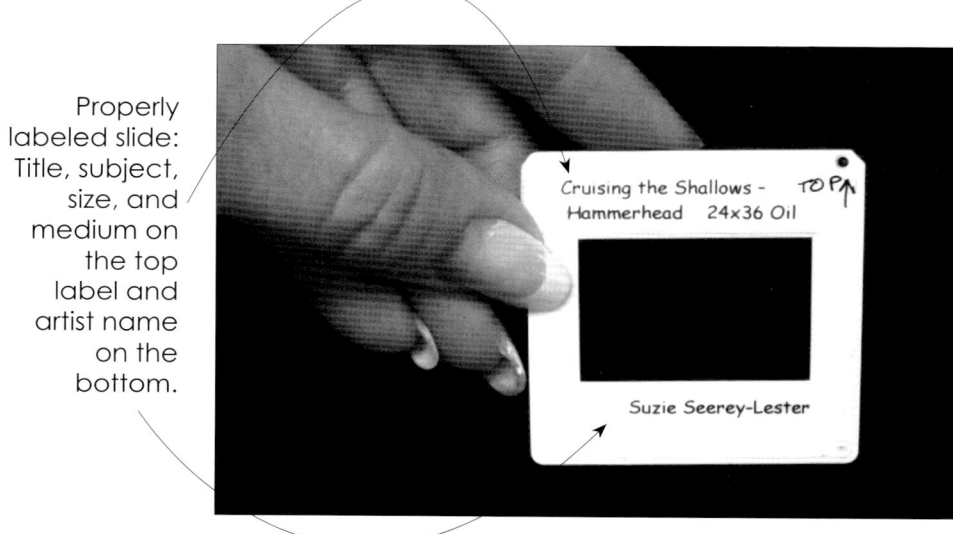

Properly labeled slide: Title, subject, size, and medium on the top label and artist name on the bottom.

Oh no. No one in my area is making slides anymore, and the show is requiring a slide; what do I do now?

We have found a few sources on the Internet that will take the digital, or 35 mm prints and convert them to slides. **DPI Art Services** is a full service company that can take digital photos, scans, convert digital photos to slides, just to name a few of their services. Their number is 1 888-721-3259 and their web site is **www.dpiartservices.com**. We have also used **ColorSlide.com** and found them to be very quick, cost-efficient and the slides came out perfectly. You can reach them at **www.colorslide.com,** 614-866-4376. Remember the results are only as good as the image that you send them, so make sure it is the best!

Transparencies

The reason you would want a transparency *tranny* would be for licensing purposes, and larger reproductions, where they need a sharp accurate image to work from. For example; to create limited edition prints, or insertion into a magazine or book, these would require *trannies*, from which scans can be made. Some magazines will require a *tranny*, others may accept digital reproductions. You must take your artwork to a professional photographer to have a *tranny* made. This is not something that you can make easily yourself. Be sure to have a color bar and/or a gray scale printed on the tranny. The gray scale and color bars are used when the piece is printed, to insure that you have accurate colors and values on the reproduction. You can have different size *trannies* produced. 4x5 or 8x10. Depending on how it is to be used, will determine the size. Be sure to view the *tranny* thru a loop to make sure there are no *speculars* (white dots produced by light bouncing off textured paintings). This is particularly relevant to oil paintings or impasto acrylics. If you have *speculars*, the photographer needs to re-shoot the *tranny*, or compensate in the processing. Again, do not varnish your painting before you have it photographed. *Trannies* are expensive they can run from $85.00 to $200.00 depending on the size and the photographer. You only need a *tranny* for specific projects. It is also important that the *trannies* are color corrected by your supplier. This will effect the cost.

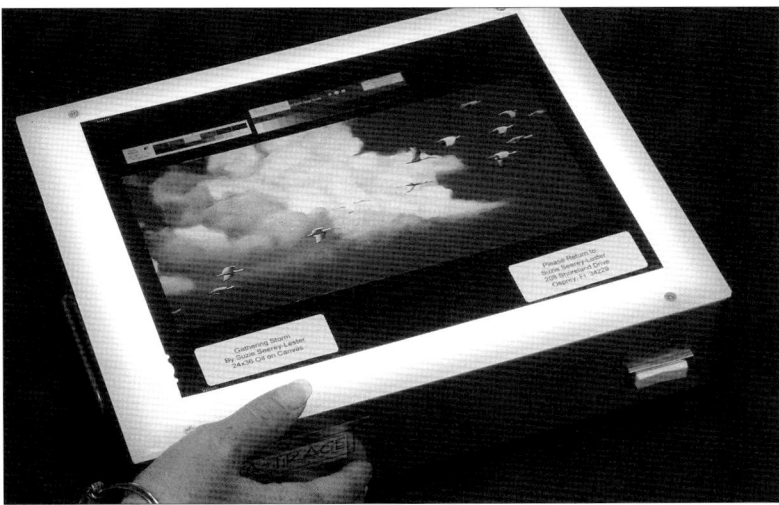

Properly labeled transparency on a light box. You can see the gray scale and the color bar that the photographer added to the transparency.

Review:

- Use a professional photographer whenever possible.
- Photograph the painting yourself properly.
- Remove the painting from the frame before photographing.
- Photograph against a black background with nothing else in view.
- Fill the screen with your image.
- Make sure the camera is parallaxed and focused.
- Do not varnish the painting before taking a photograph.
- Make photo prints, attach a label, and file under the WC#.
- Make a back up CD with the photos listed by WC#.
- Make a contact sheet for the CD and an additional copy for the Contact Sheet Book.
- Take slides, put in sleeves, and file in a three ring binder.
- Follow directions for a juried show.
- If you require a tranny, file it by name in a manila folder in a file cabinet.

Chapter 4

Framing your artwork

The Final Touch to Make Your Painting Great

You have photographed the painting, now varnish it before it can be framed. Of course there are several options for varnishing.

Varnishing Acrylic Paintings

Because acrylic paintings dry so quickly, they can be varnished almost immediately after signing your name! We have found that *Krylon Crystal Clear* is the best finish to use. Take the painting outdoors, in a well ventilated area, in an upright position. Spray the *Crystal Clear* about 9 to 12 inches from the painting in a side to side motion, then an up and down motion. Repeat this motion; move down and across the painting. Do not let it drip (you are too close) or form pools. Repeat the up and down, then side by side motion again. This should fully cover the painting. Look at it from the side to see if you have missed any obvious spots. Repeat if necessary. Let your painting dry for a few minutes. *Crystal Clear* does dry fast, but you don't want any smudges, cat hair, or dust to attach itself to your painting. Now it is ready to frame.

Varnishing Oil Paintings

Oil paintings are generally too wet to varnish upon completion. A light or re-touch varnish can be applied after the painting dries to the touch, and the final varnish should be done at least one year after the painting is completed, to allow full drying time for the oils.

There are several different methods for varnishing oil paintings. The old masters used a retouch varnish on the paintings, which would allow them to go back and "retouch" their pieces if necessary. This will bring all the values together and eliminate any "flat" or "dull" spots. Allow the oil paint to dry before attempting to varnish. Once it is dry to the touch, spray the painting with *Damar Retouch Varnish*. This will be applied in the same manner, as the *Crystal Clear* is applied, in an up and down and side-to-side motion. In an ideal world we suggest that you do a final Damar (Gloss or Matt) varnish at least six months to a year after the painting is completed. Preferably this should be brushed on. Unfortunately, with the pressure of deadlines today this final varnish is hardly ever done.

Another method to varnish an oil painting is to use *Liquin* on the piece. Once the painting is dry, put some *Liquin* on a paper palette, making sure that you apply it thinly and evenly over the painting. This will eliminate all the dull areas and bring the values into line. Now take a soft paper towel, in a circular motion, lightly rub the *Liquin* off the painting. This leaves just a very fine coat of protection. *Liquin* will dry overnight, but again, keep it away from anything that might stick to it like, fur, feathers, dust, etc. for a few days. Never, never varnish the painting in the frame.

Now It Is Ready to Frame

The painting is varnished and a frame has been selected. Take the frame and lay it face down on a hard surface covered with a soft cloth. You don't want to scratch the frame or the painting. Now lay the painting into the rabbet of the frame, and secure it by using mirror clips secured by a screw (using an electric drill or electric screwdriver, makes the job easier and faster). This is the best method for stretched canvas paintings. Mirror clips are easy to find at any hardware store and come in several different sizes, and depths. Purchase at least three different sizes (distance between the top and bottom of the clip) depending on if you are framing canvas or panel, and how deep the frame is. Make sure the screws are not too long so they do not puncture the other side of the frame. We use mirror clips ¼" and *Phillips Flat Sheet Metal Zinc Screw* 8 x ½ that we pick up from the local **Ace Hardware**.

Using a Point Driver Gun

Another method, which is faster and very secure, is to use a picture framing point driver. This tool is similar to a staple gun. Load the point driver with, you guessed it, points, push the nose of the driver against the frame, and pull the lever. A short point is driven into the wood, above the painting, securing it from moving. Drive points all the way around the painting to keep it tight into the frame. This method will only work if there is space between the back of the painting (board or canvas) and the frame, for the point to be driven in. In the case of a canvas that is higher than the frame, you will need to use mirror clips or some other method to secure it. A point driver is an inexpensive tool, which will help the framing job go quicker.

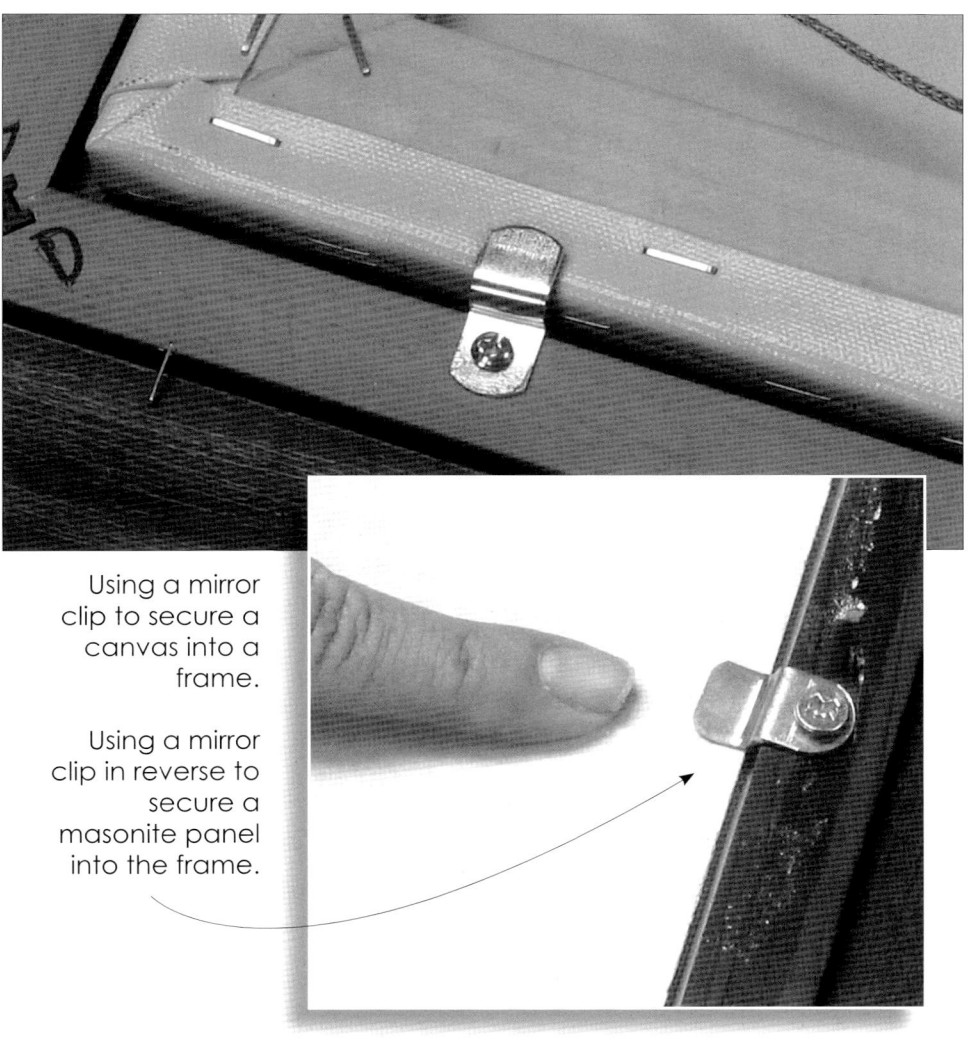

Using a mirror clip to secure a canvas into a frame.

Using a mirror clip in reverse to secure a masonite panel into the frame.

Properly labeled finished piece, with painting label, copyright label, and notice label.

Use a point driver to secure the masonite panel into the frame.

A close-up view of the points which secure the painting into the frame.

Measure out the length of wire that you will need for the back of the painting.

Example of a small "D" ring used on a small frame. The rings come in several sizes. Choose the size that works with the weight of your frame.

Framing

What kind of frame will work best on your piece? One way to find out is to take your piece to the local framer and discuss options available. The framer will want your business, and will select the best frame for the painting. Framers are professionals and are trained and knowledgeable about mats and moldings. Trust them, they usually are very creative and helpful. They can also be a great asset to you because as they frame your work, they may show it to others, or they may have clients that would be interested in your type of work. Your local framer will be a great source with whom to network.

 The key is, don't purchase ugly frames in order to save money. There are many economical stock frames available at very reasonable prices. An attractive frame will make a mediocre painting look good; a hideous frame will make a great painting look horrible. Investigate frames on the Internet. Talk to other artists and find out what types of frames they use, and where they purchase them. What type of market are you trying to reach?

When selecting frames you want to find at least a few different styles that complement the work. Find one or two companies that have a line of different types and colors and stick with that company. Obviously if you choose frames in standard sizes, i.e. 9x12, 11x14, 12x16, 24x36 etc., it makes life easier. However, many of us prefer to paint odd sizes. If you paint on an *"odd"* size panel or canvas, a custom frame must be ordered, which may be costly.

Gold and sliver frames that are 4" to 6" wide provide a classic look. Distressed wooden frames will enhance more rustic paintings. Try to select lighter colored frames, to flatter the painting. Darker frames have the effect of closing in on paintings, making them appear to be smaller. The wider the frame, the more significant the painting becomes. Select a frame color that complements the colors in your painting. For example if you have a misty, rainy scene, a silver frame may pull out the grays, where a gold frame may overpower the colors. The frame you choose is critical to the success of your painting.

The Price of Frames

The price you pay for frames is very important to your bottom line (profit). Find frames that are good quality, will complement your work, and are a good value. For many years we have been using **JFM Enterprises**. They have excellent quality frames for a good price. One frame in particular from **JFM** is only $27.00 for an 8x10, and it looks as though it is worth four times as much. Check out local art companies, like **Dick Blick**, **Graphic Dimensions** and **Michaels**. They have standard size frames that are inexpensive. Again, stick with the wider frames (4"–6") in the lighter colors. Choose wisely.

When deciding on a frame, consider the retail price of the painting. You don't want to put a $200.00 frame on a piece you will sell for $100.00. If the frame is more valuable than the painting, you may have a difficult time getting the marked-up price. Remember you want to make a profit on your frames, you are not giving them away with the painting, they are part of the cost of goods. Framing is the most important factor in presenting your work.

Custom Frames

You have a masterpiece and want a special frame to make it that much more unique. If it is an unusual size, or the painting commands a high price, a custom frame will be necessary. Now is the time to talk to a professional framer.

Visit several framers in your area and find the one that you can build a working relationship with. One framer may be more creative than the other, one may understand your needs better. A professional framer will take in consideration the size, the colors that you have used, the retail value, and maybe even the subject to create that "special" frame. Use several stock frame moldings together to make a wider frame. Add a gold filet or a linen liner, depending on the painting. Use your creativity as well as the knowledge of the framer to create that perfect frame. A custom frame will be much more costly than a standard frame, and the wait may be up to 10 weeks to receive the frame. This is where the relationship with the framer comes in handy. They may have some molding left over from another project that will work, and can do their magic on it to have a wonderful frame ready in a short period of time. Framers know the good designs that have been used for years and what will work on your type of artwork properly, using acid free material and the proper glass that will enhance the work and protect it for years. A good eye for framing cannot be taught, so trust the professional to help you make the choices to produce an elegant well-balanced piece of art.

It is also important to check out the frames normally displayed in your gallery of choice. Your work needs to be in keeping and stand out amongst the other art.

Order your Frames Ahead of Time

Plan ahead when ordering frames. Most frame companies will have a season, where most of their frames are sold out, and anything that you order will be back ordered for months. Plan to order one or two styles of frames in a few standard sizes in which you normally paint. For example, order two 8x10s in style XYZ, and three 9x12s in style WXY, and two 9x12s in XYZ styles. The frames are in your studio, now paint to those sizes. Frame companies will have standard size frames, which will accommodate standard size canvas or panel. If you like unusual size paintings, for example, 18 x 36, expect to go to the expense of a custom frame. Allow time for the framer to produce the frame. Don't expect them to create a frame in two days. Plan ahead.

Framing Under Glass

Watercolors and pastels need special handling and should be framed under glass to preserve them. There are several different types of glass to choose from, again depending on your needs, as well as what the clients want and your budget. Ultra-violet light is the most damaging element to your artwork. It can cause the colors to fade, damage the paper and even cause it to yellow and become brittle. To protect your hard work, choose the glass that will most protect the art. There are basically three choices in glass. First is normal glass with no protection. You can see your work; it will be protected from the rain and dust, but not from light. The second glass is *"conservation glass,"* which prevents over 95+% of the damaging light from coming in contact with the work. This is a medium cost glass and is suggested as the minimum that should be used to protect the artwork. There are different brand names; just ask for conservation glass. The third type glass is called *"museum quality glass."* This has all the protection of the conservation glass, and it has a unique quality of being non-reflective as well. With this type of glass you will be able to clearly see your image, as if it it was sitting in a pocket of air, or a frame without glass.

Paper the Back of the Frame

To *"finish"* off your framing, paper the back of the frame. Traditionally, brown paper is glued to the back of the frame, and a slit or opening (some people cut one corner off) is created to allow the canvas to breathe. This slit is not necessary if masonite is being framed. Measure out your paper about 1/8" from the edge, apply double-sided tape or glue (hot glue works well, just don't over-glue) making sure not to have any glue or tape outside of the paper. Use a glue that is relatively quick to dry. Place the paper on the frame, and weigh it down, if necessary until the glue dries. Now use a piece of left over paper to create a sleeve (6 x 10) to hold the Certification of Original Artwork, Care and Handling, and your Bio. Glue or tape three sides to the bottom back of the painting, leaving the top of the sleeve open to insert the paperwork. Now the painting is ready to wire.

To wire the back of the painting, screw the *D-ring* hanger (also available in different sizes at the local hardware store) about 6 to 8 inches from the top of the frame on both sides. Depending on the size of the painting, measure the wire (40 lb. wire at least) so it fits securely across the frame with at least two inches on each side. Loop the wire through the first *D-ring*, wrap it on itself, secure it, pull it tight, and secure the second side. When hung, the wire should be at least one to two inches below the fop of the frame. That way you will not see any hardware when the painting is hanging on the wall.

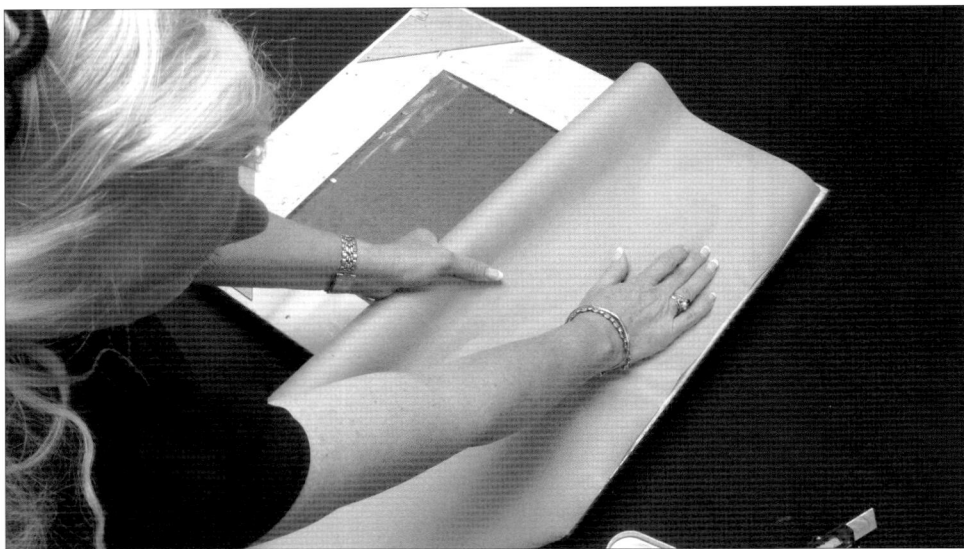

Measure out and cut a length of brown paper a little larger than your frame.

Tape all four sides of the back of the frame with double sided tape. You can also use rubber cement.

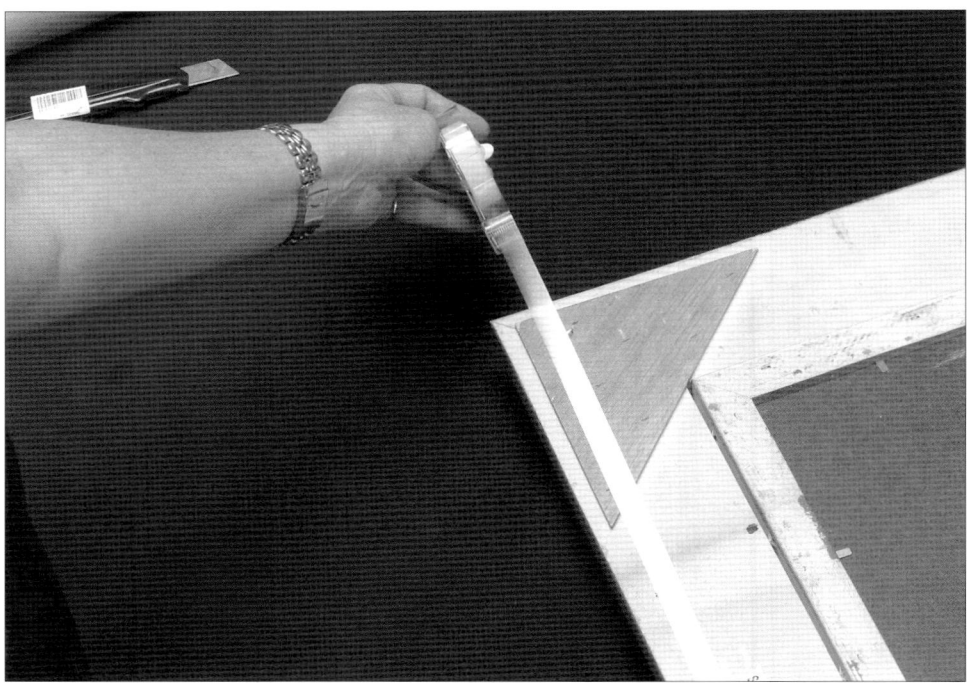

Place pre cut brown paper on top of double sided tape or rubber cement and press into place.

Cut away and remove any excess brown paper.

Corner of a paper backed frame, after being trimmed.

After the paper is in place, now you can add the "D" ring and wire.

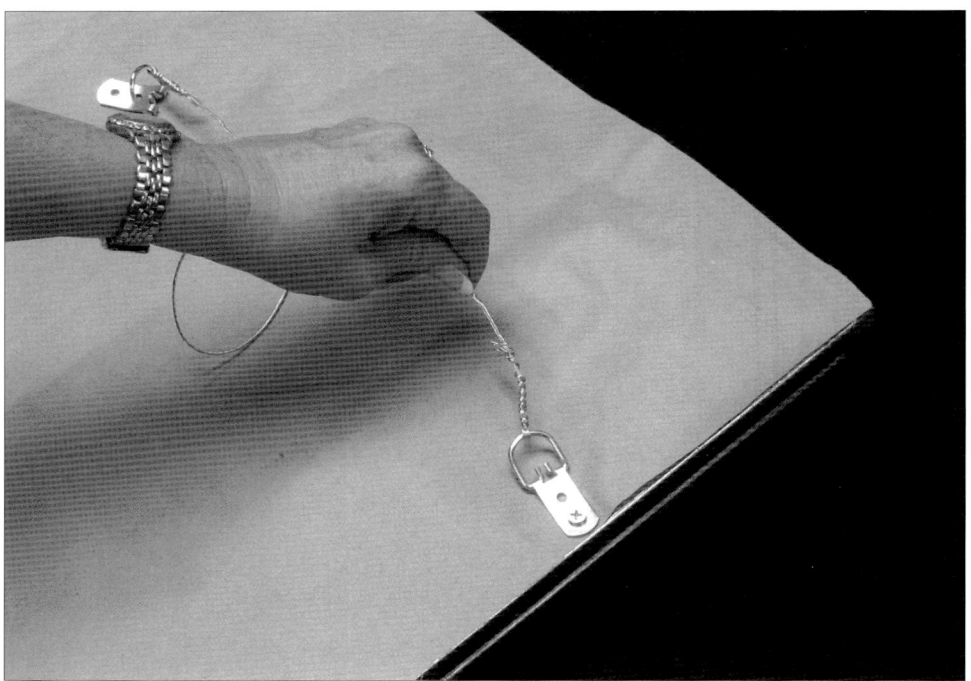

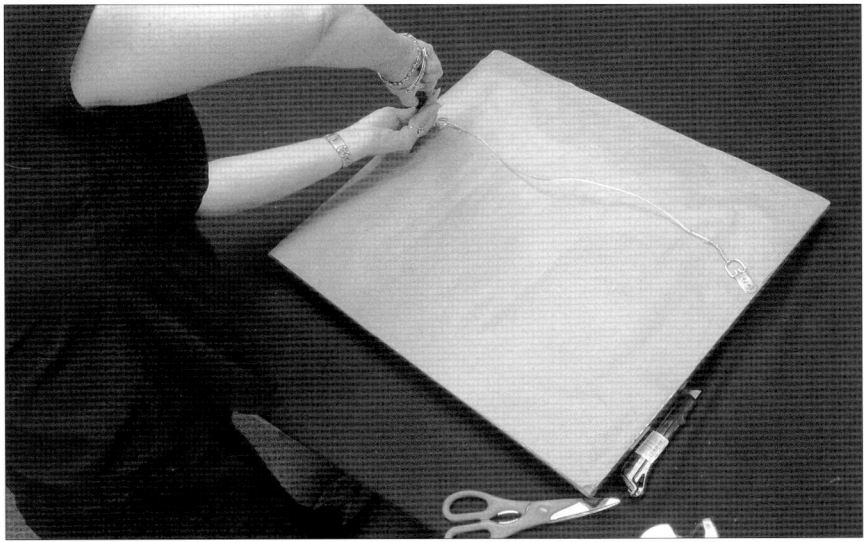

Securing the final "D" ring and wire, make sure the wire is tight and does not show above the frame when it is hanging.

Cut an extra sheet of brown paper to add to the back as a sleeve to hold your documents.

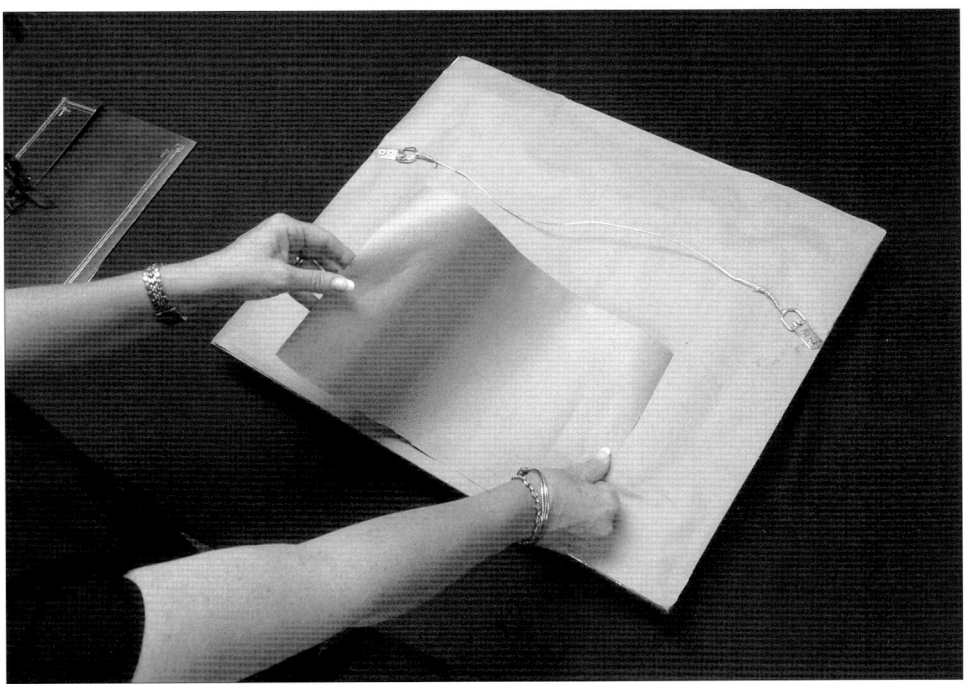

The documents that go in the sleeve: Folder to hold documents, Bill of Sale, your Bio, Care and Handling, Certificate of Original Artwork, your Tri-Fold Brochure, Business Card, Thank You Card and Fine Art Registration Card.

Place all documents in the folder, and slip inside the sleeve on the back of the painting.

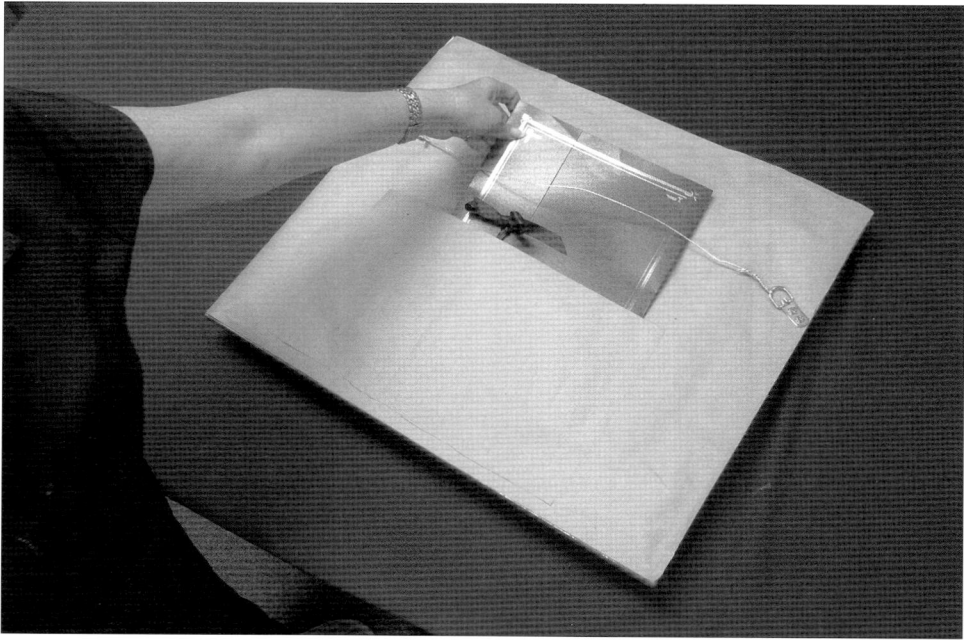

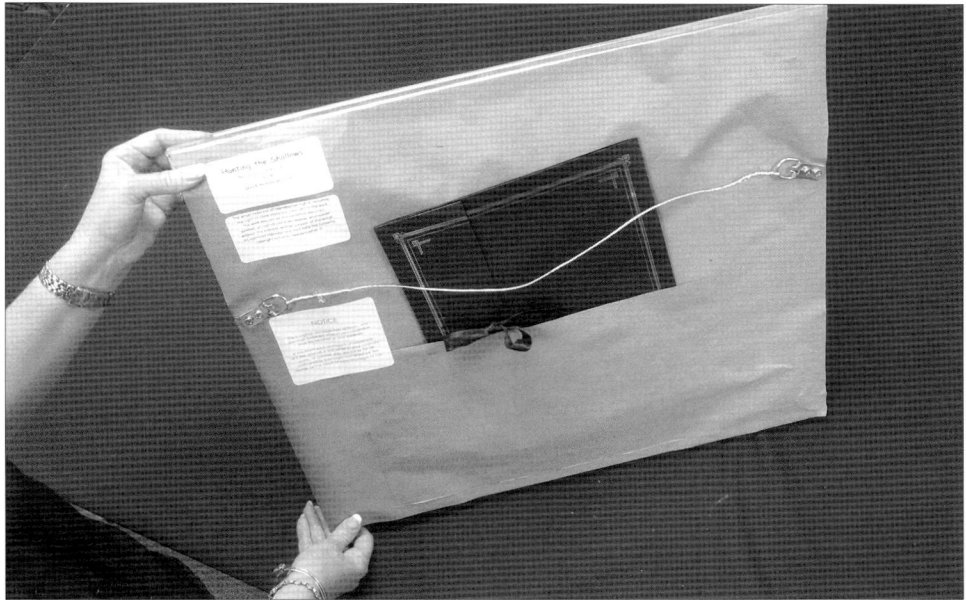

Add your three labels to the back of the paper. The original labels are still on the back of the panel under the paper.

The final touch, add the name plate to the frame.

The final touch for your painting is a brass nameplate. Once the title of your painting has been determined, order the nameplate from a company like **Allisons**. They come in different sizes and styles, so choose a style that you like and use it on every painting. The title on the first line is the largest type, your name on the second line, in smaller type, and a third line, if available, have the size and medium in the smaller type. These can be glued, nailed or screwed straight onto the frame. Place it in the middle of the bottom section of the frame. This adds the final professional polish to your piece.

Review:

- Varnish your painting before framing it.
- Choose a frame that complements your painting. A good frame will make your painting stand out; a bad one will hide it.
- Plan ahead and order your frames early.
- Frame your painting securing it into the frame using mirror clips or a point driver.
- Frame under proper glass.
- Paper the back of the frame.
- Create a sleeve for the paperwork.
- Put a wire on the back of the frame.
- Attach the brass nameplate on the frame.

Chapter 5

The business side of things

There are lots of books on how to market your work and get into a gallery. This is not one of them. This chapter will cover things to do after you have been accepted into a gallery, or have a good list of clients to work with. These are *extras* to provide the gallery to help them sell your work. You have invested a lot of time and money to get into a gallery or show, and want that important investment to start paying off in the form of sales. So anything that can be done to help the gallery sell your piece, is beneficial and very productive.

First impressions are very important. The painting is framed so it looks elegant, expensive, and a valuable asset. It has been photographed, and everything is ready for the photos to be sent to galleries and collectors. Complete the package by putting your best foot forward. A few more details need to be completed first.

Start a Procedures Manual

You don't want to be typing labels for the rest of your life, so at some point, an assistant (even on a part time basis) needs to be hired. Start to write a *Procedures Manual* as forms or concepts are created. When you hire an assistant, half of the work is done. The *Procedures Manual* can be an instructional manual to teach any new employees your business. Use a large binder with dividers for every task/concept/form. Write directions and an explanation of what to do for every duty created, for example:

Original Information Sheet.
1. Fill out form at the start of each painting.
2. Check off each item when completed.
3. Attach a photo of painting to this sheet.
4. File in binder. File the Original Information Sheet and the explanation in the Procedures Manual. Do this for everything, including making brochures, setting up inventory, burning CD's. Do not omit anything. As you create the task, copy it into the binder. Now any one that comes in to assist, can easily see what is expected on each process.

Copyright

Under current copyright laws, your copyright is secured automatically when the piece is created, as long as it is your original work, and has some degree of creativity and is in a tangible form. In other words, the idea or concept underlying the painting is not protected by copyright, only your expression of the idea is covered. So someone can see your work, be inspired by it and express the ideas embodied in your work, in their own work as long as their expression of the idea is different. However, their work, can not be *substantially similar* to yours. If it is, then it infringes on your rights and you can prevent them from showing, selling or reproducing the *infringing* work. There are many old wives tales about changing, 5%, or six elements or so many colors, etc.; they all are nonsense and have no basis in the law. There is no magical safe harbor for the amount one can copy when it comes to copyright.

When the original is signed, be sure to include the © (copyright symbol) after your signature. The notice or visually perceptible copies should contain three elements: The copyright symbol ©, the year of completion, and the name of the owner of the copyright, for example; sign your painting: *Suzie Seerey-Lester © 2007*. This will prevent anyone from claiming that they did not know the work was protected or who the copyright owner is.

How Long Does Copyright Protection Last?

If the work was created in 1978 or later, it will be protected for the life of the artist, plus 70 years after the artist's death. This means your estate can collect royalties for seventy years after your death.

Many works created before January 1, 1978 but after 1922, are now covered by the statute and given federal copyright protection. Please consult with the copyright office if you have any work created before January 1, 1978, and would like to know more specific information, see the *Copyright Office Circular* 15a (**www.copyright.gov**). Works published in the USA before 1923 are in the public domain and anyone is free to copy them.

The copyright law works for artists in two ways, one to protect *your* work, and the other is to protect someone else's work from *you*. This means your art must be *your* original art. Do not copy photos out of books and magazines. Do not copy other artist's work. Published works in books, magazines, and on the internet, etc., are copyright protected and you must have written permission to use someone else's work. It is imperative that your work be original. Photographers have copyright protection on the photos that they have published in the books and magazines that are viewed by thousands of other people. If you copy any part of the photograph in your work, the photographer can sue you for copyright infringement. There are several famous photographers who have staff that do nothing else but look for artists using their photographs, and then sue the artist. We cannot stress this enough; take your own photographs, and use only your own photographs. Some of these photographers don't really care if you are a Sunday Afternoon Painting Grandmother, if you have infringed on their work, they have the right to sue. You want the copyright laws to protect your originals, so please respect the laws that protect the photographers and other artists.

Registration with the *US Copyright office* is very important and is highly recommended. If your work is infringed upon, whether it had been registered before the infringement or not, will in many cases, determine if you have an economically viable claim. If your work was registered prior to the infringement, you are entitled to have the infringer pay your attorney fees and statutory damages, which can be as high as $150,000.00 per infringement. If not, you are limited to the infringer's profits or your losses. In many such instances your attorney fees will exceed the potential recovery. Registration is very easy and not expensive. You can download the form, VA, from the *Copyright Office* website: (**www.copyright.gov**). If you have a number of unpublished works, those you have not offered for sale as prints or other form of multiples, can be registered all on one application as a collection, for a single $45.00 fee. For details, look at *Copyright Office Circulars 40 and 40a,* (**www.copyright.gov**). Send the package of the application, check and copies of the works to:
    Library of Congress
    Copyright Office
    101 Independence Avenue S.E.,
    Washington, DC 20559-6000

Your registration becomes effective on the day that the Copyright Office receives your application, payment and copies in acceptable form. Overnight the package, and require a signature, so you have proof of the date received. If your submission is in order, a *Certificate of Registration* will be sent in 4 to 5 months.

Intellectual Property Specialist

If you need an attorney that specializes in Intellectual Property (your art/paintings), we can recommend:

> **Mr. Joshua Kaufman**
> **Venable LLP**
> **575 7th Street, N.W.,**
> **Washington, DC 20004**
> **(202) 344-8538**

or contact them at **jkaufman@venable.com**. They can file the copyright documentation, provide legal council on copyrights, art law, art licensing, and if needed, sue for your protection of your copyright. They are the good guys. Be careful in choosing an attorney; you want one who is knowledgeable, honest and hard working.

Licensing Your Work

The licensing industry is a huge, and growing business. Licensing is the business of leasing the rights to your image on a product for a limited time. This is done by means of a contract (a license) for a specific product (T-shirts, etc.), for a specific time period (1 year, 5 years) for a specific territory (US only, US and Europe), for a specific fee or royalty (3% to 20% depending on the product or service). In some cases, instead of royalties the producer of the product may pay a one time flat fee. If you are interested in having work licensed, having a body of work that is acceptable to the general public would be easy to license. Do lots of homework before signing any contracts. Read licensing magazines to get ideas, or attend a licensing show to see what is available. There are lots of books on the market for licensing artwork. Again be careful, do not give away your copyright or sell yourself short.

Creating a Business Name and Licenses

If you will be doing any type of retail business, i.e. selling to clients directly, or wholesaling to a gallery, it is recommended you form a company. Get professional advice from an attorney and CPA. Look into getting a business name. Start with a fictitious business name from your state government, usually on line. This will be the name of your company. It could be *"Bright Idea Studio;"* it could be just your name. Be creative, think about the image you want to project, and come up with a name that works. Check with the *State Government (Department of State)* for their requirements. Next get a reseller's (wholesale) license, so you can purchase goods, like frames and art materials that you will be re-selling. The purpose of the reseller's license is for you to be able to purchase goods without paying tax on goods that you will be selling. For example, if you purchase a frame for $200.00 and pay the local tax of, for example 7%, turn around and add it to the cost of the painting, sell it at retail price, which will now be taxed again. There is no need to pay tax on some things that will be resold at retail, which will be taxed again. Different states call this license by different names. It could be a reseller's license, and it could be called a wholesale license; again, check with your state and county government. Set up a tax account, where the money that you have collected for tax, is deposited. This can be paid on a quarterly basis. Keep good records. Check with the State and County to see if you also need a business license, or any other license they may require. Again, it will differ with each State and County. The states usually give great assistance to new business owners, so check out your State Government's website, and your county website as well. This will only apply to you if you are selling your paintings to the retail public, charging and collecting tax. If you send the paintings to a gallery or show, they will collect the tax and pay it to the appropriate agency. A business attorney can help set up the proper accounts and corporations that are needed. They will be able to tell you whether to open an S Corp, LLC, or other specific licenses you will need.

Once you have a fictitious business name, take the certificate to your bank and open a Business Bank Account. Run all your funds thru this account. Everything that is sold will be deposited into this account; everything that is paid out (studio rent, taxes, postage, framing, art supplies, etc) needs to be paid out of this account. Once you set up the fictitious business name you will start to receive offers in the mail for credit card machines and services. Our suggestion is to work with your bank on the credit card service. Most banks will have a *"Merchant Services"* Department, which handles the needs of the business accounts. They can direct you to the credit card service company they use. It will probably have better rates (yes, you get to pay a percentage of your sales to the credit card company) and easier qualifying limits. This division of the bank will also sell you the credit card machine. If you are going to be selling at outdoor shows, we suggest you purchase a mobile wireless machine, so you can make sales in the field. The credit card service offers that you receive in the mail may have higher percentages, and, they may also tag on a monthly service fee. You may be required to do a certain level of business each month or be penalized. Work with the bank. Once the credit card service is set up you can take credit cards for sales. The money is credited directly into your business bank account (minus the pre-determined percentages and fees). It makes your job a lot easier. Some of these credit card systems will also "approve" checks. This will protect you against bounced checks, etc. Wait to get a credit card service until you are ready to sell to the public. Do not rush into getting the service. If the monthly minimum is not met, they may cancel their service making it more difficult to restart it when you are truly ready.

Someone once said your three best friends should be, an accountant, a banker and a lawyer. This is certainly true when you are starting a business. Find the business professionals that you are comfortable with and can grow with. It is appropriate to interview accountants before your start using them. Get to know the president of the bank. They can help you find a good accountant or recommend a business lawyer.

Once the business is up and running, check with the accountant about incorporating your business. This may save taxes and protect your assets.

Creating a Logo

Now create a business logo. It can be as simple as your signature, or a special font from the computer. You may want to hire a graphic design company to come up with a unique logo, and then use it on all your correspondence, business cards, post cards, and newsletter, etc. Alternatively, as an artist, perhaps you can design it yourself before passing it on to a graphic designer to clean up.

Create Your Biography

A simple one-page bio on your work as an artist is all you need. Think of it as a job resume, with one big difference, it has to be interesting. Create awareness and curiosity in your work. Tell a story, list achievements, shows, awards that you have won. How did you get interested in art? Where did you go to school? Who may have influenced your work? Have you painted in any interesting locations, like Africa or Alaska or downtown Osprey? Just starting out, with no credentials? Talk about your area and how you work; the direction your art is taking. It needs to be short and sweet, do not exceed one page. Include your address, phone numbers, e-mail address and website. Check special software packages that will help create brochures. **HP** has free software that can be downloaded. Sometimes it will be included in the tri-fold paper or brochure paper that HP offers. It is easy to create unique brochures with these software packages. You can purchase special papers from **Staples** or **Office Depot**, to make it different and unique. It should stand out from every other artist's bio. Keep a good stock of them; send them out with every painting that is sold. Hand them out at shows. Create interest. Check out **Hewlett-Packard** free software on **www.hp.com.**

Design a Website

A website is a full time salesman, 24 hours a day, who never takes a vacation, and doesn't get pregnant! Websites are not expensive, but they may bring in lots of business to you. Interview Webmasters in your area. Go to the local technical college to find whiz kids who are learning the latest technology. Talk to other artists, find out what works on their websites. What do they like best? Who do they use as a Webmaster? Who are they using to build and maintain their site? Change your paintings frequently. Find someone who is very knowledgeable about websites. You want your name at the top of the list when someone is searching for your type of art. They will help you develop *key words* for phrases that will increase your ability to be found by the search engines and directories. Update these key words frequently. Again, find your *"brand"* or unique niche and capitalize on it. If you have lots of people linked to your website, some search engines will rate your site higher than someone with fewer links. Ask people that you know to link to your site, if they are appropriate. Join other organizations that have web sites such as *Artists for Conservation, Society of Animal Artists*, etc. Place your links on their sites, and theirs on yours. Build a page with these organizations. The more places you are, the better opportunity to be seen on the Web. Some magazines may offer a page on their site for their clients that purchase ad space in the magazine. Have your Webmaster add a counter, so you can see how many *"hits"* or people have visited your site. Update the site, with sold banners across pieces that have sold. If the piece is at a gallery, have that listed under the painting so prospective buyers can contact the gallery directly.

Do not upset the gallery by leaving them off the site. It is not a good business practice to be competing with your own gallery. Have the website linked to other websites, organizations, shows, and galleries that you belong to. Make the website easy to navigate. Attach your e-mail, so if someone has a question, they can contact you directly. Have an electronic newsletter, attached to the website, include the schedule as well as any shows that you will be participating in so clients can meet you. Put your web address on everything, business cards, letterheads, brochures, VIP packages, (discussed later in this chapter), and the newsletters. You want to do anything to raise awareness in your paintings.

Accepting Commissions

A commission is a request for a piece of art that a client wants you to create just for them. Different people view commissions in different ways. Some artists will allow the client to dictate to the smallest detail of what to paint. Other artists will ask the client what subject they would like, and create the piece from there. However you decide to handle commissions, it is important to ask for a nonrefundable deposit, up front, and the balance due upon receipt of the artwork. This will take care of a few things. First, is the client really interested in a commission, and willing to pay the fee? Some clients will talk about a commission all day long, but never really intend to pay for the paintings. Second, by receiving a deposit up front, the client has committed to the painting. If the client backs out, you will keep the nonrefundable deposit. Third, you now have the funds to purchase paint, canvases, frames, and have photographs taken. Once the client has seen the finished commission, if he is pleased with it, he will pay the balance. If there are a few things that need to be reworked to make him happy, do so, then present the painting again. Finally, if they do not like the painting, or it just was not what they envisioned, which can happen, you have the option of keeping the nonrefundable deposit, creating a whole new piece for them, or refunding their deposit. By keeping the original painting, and creating a new one for the client, you are free to sell the original for the full retail price. As with any piece of art that you create, do your best work, and be proud of what you do. When you are half way through the painting, visit the client, show them the piece, or show them photographs of the artwork at that stage. When the client is happy with the completed artwork, you collect the remaining balance.

Keep a Scrapbook

You made it into a local newspaper or a trade magazine. Keep the article in a special scrapbook of your achievements. If you are accepted into a show, or receive an award, keep it in your scrapbook. When the newsletter is created, keep a copy of it. In later years, you can use some of these items in future newsletters or the VIP program (later in this chapter). If a magazine wants to know of your achievements, they are all in one place. We put all the articles in plastic sheet protectors and put the sheets in a binder. This way your original article will not be damaged, so if needed, copies can be made.

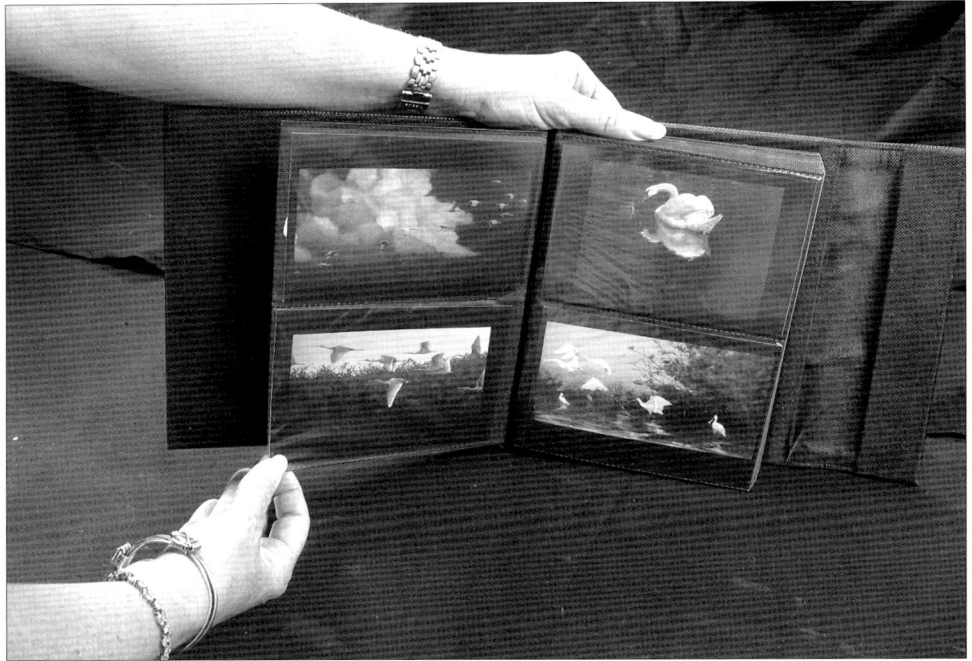

Keep a photo album of all your paintings to show to prospective clients.

Photo Album of your Paintings

Start a photo album of your artwork. This will show potential clients the scope of your work, your style and your subject matter. When meeting someone interested in seeing some of your work, have an album available. Have it on the table in your studio, available when anyone drops by to visit.

Using Software

The goal for most artists is to paint, not to try to figure out the balance sheet from the bank. The other software package that we suggest is **QuickBooks**. This is an easy to use accounting package to help keep track of invoices, taxes, inventory, etc. You can pick this up at most computer stores or office supply stores, and on line at **www.quickbooks.intuit.com.**

To make organization in the studio easy, get some software that can help with these tasks. We have been using "**Software for Artists**" for quite a while. This software makes it very easy to keep our client lists and mailing lists. You can track a patron; create multiple mailing lists; create standard price lists, and a history of shows. This software helps with marketing, and will basically get you organized. To contact them: **www.workingartist.com** or (800) 897-3758

A Painting Paragraph, with the photo, to attach to the wall next to your painting is your Silent Salesman.

Painting Paragraph

When you send the artwork to the gallery, include a short paragraph about the painting on nice paper. It can be the same information used in the VIP program. Tell a story about the painting. Point out unique things in the painting that may not be easily seen. Try to get it in a 5x8 area on the paper. Place this on a foam board or mat board. Ask the gallery to put this next to the painting. This is a sales tool; it tells a story about the painting that a client can easily read as they move thru the gallery. It is a passive way to sell your painting, or *"silent salesman."* If you are the only artist in the gallery with this *painting paragraph*, it will make your painting more noticeable and hopefully easier to sell. The gallery sales people will love it, as will the clients. If it helps you to connect with that one person, they may purchase your painting.

VIP package with a newsletter, press clippings, painting paragraph, your bio, press releases, business card, tri-fold brochure, and nice folder.

VIP Program

As your list of collectors grows, create a program designed to add impact to anything that they buy. Send the Gallery something that will cause them to remember you, above and beyond other artists they carry. Have your images in front of them for as long as possible. Give them something they will keep around for a while.

Start with good quality brochure paper, perhaps coated, which is usually heavier and thicker than copier paper. This will print better, look more professional, and show off your artwork better than plain paper. Take the photograph of your painting (get it into the computer the normal way for you, scan it in, or direct from the card or camera), and drop it into the document (in "Word" for example). Once the photo has been centered, directly below it in large type, print the title. The next line, in smaller print type: by your name. The final line should be the size and medium.

Now insert the painting paragraph that we discussed earlier in this chapter. Don't make it too long, but make it interesting. Finally on the bottom of the VIP page, have your phone number, e-mail address and website. If this process overwhelms you because you are not computer oriented, take your information to **Kinko's, Sir Speedy, Staples** or **Office Depot** and they will help you create your VIP sheet.

Send the new VIP sheet to the client or gallery in a nice folder, or a special binder. Include your newsletter. If you use a binder, it will hold all the sheets, and make it easy to show to prospective buyers or their friends and relatives, who may also be potential buyers. Every time you complete a new painting, create a VIP sheet, send it out in a large envelope, and do not fold it. Yes it will cost a little more for the envelope and the postage, but the impression that you will give the client or the gallery will be well worth the expense. Follow up a week after sending it out to make sure your client or gallery has received the latest VIP sheet. Answer any questions they may have.

Take any opportunity you can to be in front of a client and succeed. Remember, winners will do what losers won't. Be a winner.

A quarterly newsletter that you send out to all contacts to let them know what you have been accomplishing during the last few months.

Newsletter

Let the clients and galleries know what you have been up to. Create a monthly or quarterly newsletter. This can be sent out electronically via e-mail or in a hard paper format. Like the VIP program, you want impact. Have lots of color in the newsletter and photos of you and your paintings. If you have gone on any painting trips, let them know. Tell stories of the trip; show the paintings created on the trip. This could be a simple trip to the state park in your area, that is only five minutes away, but play it up. Have someone photograph you while you are painting. If you have received any awards, put it in the newsletter. If you have been in the paper, provided donations to a charity, given or taken a class, put it in the newsletter. Most importantly give information on shows, providing the dates and times. A one-man/woman show, or an open studio show you are having should be definitely included. The more interesting things you tell people about you and your paintings, the more they will identify with you and hopefully want to buy your art. Keep your name in front of the clients and the galleries, in the hope that when they want a painting, they will call you first. The newsletter is an essential marketing tool.

Open Studio

If you have the room, a once-a-year "Open Studio Show and Sale" is highly recommended. Clients and potential clients always enjoy seeing artists at work. Send out post cards to all your clients and galleries; give them the dates and times of the show. Order postcards via the Internet and have them delivered in a matter of a few days. We have used **Modern Post Cards** for years and have been extremely pleased with the results. You can contact them at **www.modernpostcards.com**.

Send the post cards out about three weeks prior to the show. Have the date, time, and the fact that your paintings will be FOR SALE. Have an open studio on a weekend, either a Friday evening and all day Saturday, or all day Saturday and Sunday. Provide refreshments, which could be as simple as coffee and cake, or if you chose, wine, beer, sodas and finger food. Have the wine and beer in one area, or serve it as they come in, so they can enjoy their wine as they view all your wonderful work. Have the food in another area, away from the paintings, in a small area that they cannot cluster and hang around.

Have a guest book at the entrance of the studio for guests to sign and make comments. You now have an instant mailing list to use next year. If your studio is attached or adjacent to the house, use the living area of the house as an additional display area, putting your work on easels as well as the walls.

On each painting have a sticker with a number. Then type your *Catalog List*. List your paintings by the assigned number. Show the title, size, medium and original price. Give this printed list to each person as they walk in. If they are interested in a piece, they can easily see the title, and the price listed by the assigned number. Remember; do not undercut the gallery prices. Be sure to collect the proper amount of sales tax. When a sale is made have the customer fill out name, address and phone number, in a two part sales form book. You fill in the item sold and the amount. Include any shipping or extras, if necessary, and then add the tax for your area. If they are using a credit card, note it on the form, and run the card. Staple the credit card receipt to the customer's copy of the sales sheet. If they are paying by check, note the check number on the sales sheet. Give the client one copy of the sales sheet; you keep the other copy. Now add all these names to your client list.

A few days after the studio show, send out thank you notes to anyone who made a purchase. If they bought a pack of $5.00 cards, or a $5,000.00 painting, they need to be thanked. Your customer will remember this small gesture, and hopefully will want to come back again next year.

Review:

- Create a *Procedures Manual* for all your forms/concepts/procedures.
- Put the copyright symbol © on every painting after your signature and date.
- If you are going to publish or license your image, register it with the US Copyright Office in Arlington, VA.
- Do not copy photographs or other artists' works from books and magazines; they are copyright © protected.
- License your work.
- Create a business name and logo.
- Establish a business license from your state.
- Create your Biography.
- Accept Commissions.
- Keep a Scrapbook.
- Create a Website.
- Use software to help your business.
- Print a *Painting Paragraph* for each painting.
- Create a *VIP Sheet* on every painting.
- Send out a *Newsletter* periodically.
- Host an *Open Studio Sale*.

Chapter 6

Consigning your artwork

Consignment Agreement

Yeah! A gallery has agreed to accept several of your paintings on a consignment basis. Now what do you do? Create a *Consignment Agreement*. This is a contract between you and the gallery/show allowing them to hang your painting for a specific period of time, and if they sell it during that time, they will pay you a commission based on the agreement. State the length of the consignment, so they know how long they will be able to keep your piece. Clearly show the retail and wholesale value of the piece. What percentage are you working on with this gallery? What is the value of the piece to the public? Include any specific information that is unique to you. This is a contract between you and the gallery. You still own this piece, until the gallery pays you the wholesale price. You will always own the copyright, and they cannot use the image unless you give them permission. If the piece is damaged, or modified while consigned to the gallery, the gallery is responsible for the repair or the wholesale value of the piece.

All of the above needs to be covered in the *Consignment Agreement*, so there will be no questions later. If the piece is lost in shipping to the gallery, you are responsible. If it is lost on the way back, the gallery is responsible. Who is paying for the shipping? The general rule is, the artist pays to ship the painting to the gallery; the gallery pays to ship it back or to the next location, as long as the painting has exceeded the agreed upon consignment period. This needs to be discussed prior to shipping any paintings.

Using your letterhead, create the *Consignment Agreement*. Put the consignee's name and address and phone number at the top. This is the gallery or show where the painting is to be on display, the date the painting was sent, and the period of the consignment. This will differ at each gallery and is something that you have to discuss. The usual period is 12 months, but can be more or less depending on you and the Gallery's requirements. Obviously if the piece is going to a show or an exhibition, it will be required to be there for the duration of that show. An example of the typical *Consignment Agreement* is shown here. Discuss what the commission split will be with you and the gallery, or show. Normally it is 60/40 (yes, you get the 60%), or 50/50.

Bright Idea Studio
1221 South Adams
Osprey, Fl 34229

(222) 222-2222
brightideastudio@aol.com
www.BrightIdeaStudio.com

Consignment Agreement

Due Artist   Recommended

WC# Retail	Title	Size	Medium	Wholesale
10/07	Morning stroll $1,950.00	8x16	oil	$1170.00
11/07	Morning Preen (Ibis)	9x12	acrylic	$900.00 $1,500.00

Terms of Consignment:

1. From January 1 – December 31, 2007.
2. Artist to be paid in US Dollars, net 30, day.
3. Paintings are framed and ready to hang. Do Not Varnish or use Liquin on any paintings without first contacting and getting written permission from artist.
4. This is original, damage-free artwork. Any damage sustained while in your possession must be repaired at your expense. In the event such damage is un-repairable or if this artwork is lost while in your custody, care, or control, you are liable for all costs and/or damages sustained by the owner as the result of such damage or loss.
5. The artist reserves all reproduction rights, including the right to claim statutory copyright in the work. The work may not be photographed sketched, painted or reproduced in any manner whatsoever without the express, written consent of the artist. All approved reproductions shall bare the following copyright notice by © *your name here*.

_____   _____
Gallery Signature   Date

Please sign and return one copy upon receipt of the painting to: Bright Idea Studio
1221 S Adams, Osprey, Fl 34229 (222) 222-2222

However, some shows only require 30%. This needs to be agreed upon before sending the painting. Fill in both the Wholesale Price (what you get paid) and the Recommended Retail Price (what the piece should sell for) so there is no question about the fees. Any special requirements, i.e., for the *Summer Show* only, or any special things that have been agreed upon prior to the shipment, should be included. At the bottom of the agreement should be the all-important copyright disclaimer:

Copyright © Disclaimer

The artist reserves all reproduction rights, including the right to claim statutory copyright in the work. The work may not be photographed, sketched, painted, or reproduced in any manner whatsoever without the express written consent of the artist. All approved reproductions shall bear the following copyright notice: © (put your name here)

Now make four copies. One copy goes in that gallery file, one copy goes in the *Consignment Binder* and two copies go with the painting. The gallery needs to sign one copy and return it to you. The Gallery keeps the second copy for their files. Be sure to follow up and make sure this is done. This is important. If the piece is damaged or lost while consigned, and you do not have the signed paperwork you may have problems collecting on any loss. Once the signed copy is returned, it goes in the gallery file. The *Consignment Agreement* is used every time, because it documents the actual painting, and agreed upon prices to be consigned.

Dealing Direct with Clients

If a client you do not know contacts you and wants to purchase an original, do not send the painting to them until their check clears their bank. There are too many scams affecting artists, where a painting is purchased with stolen or fraudulent checks/credit cards/money orders. Protect yourself, by being cautious.

There are a few ethical things you may have to deal with during your career. Here are a few common situations that often occur: A painting, hanging in a gallery, nears the end of the agreed consignment period. A private buyer wants to purchase the painting and contacts you. What do you do? Get the painting back from the Gallery? It could mean more money in your pocket in the short term, but in the long term it will damage your relationship with the gallery. We suggest that you tell the buyer that the painting is currently at XYZ Gallery, and you will contact the gallery directly and advise them of the client's intent. Get all the buyer's information, and contact the Gallery. Normally this situation is caused by a collector hoping to buy the paintings for less and avoid paying the Gallery's commission. You can do one of two things; deduct a percentage from the retail price, and sell to the client for less, or tell the gallery what you are doing and pay them their 40% of the selling price. In this way everyone is happy. Alternatively, and this is perhaps better, allow the gallery to give the client a discount and split that with them. Galleries are usually happy to do this and clients get the break they want. Most important you have maintained a good relationship with the gallery.

You have just returned from a show, and are contacted by a customer that you saw at the show. This client now wants to purchase the painting he saw during your exhibition. (Some buyers think that they can purchase the painting for less after the show.) The best way to proceed is to offer the client the piece, for the same price that it was displayed at the show. If the client purchases the painting, send the commission to the show. Again, this is a win-win for everyone. The show sees that you are ethical and will respect you for this. A time period of two months after the show is sufficient, unless the show organizers have specified a longer period in their agreement. This might help you get invited back to that show.

A client of the gallery calls you and wants to purchase a painting directly from you. This could be a painting that you currently have in your studio. They may have seen it on your website. If you know the client is a regular at the gallery, or you know they purchase from that gallery, do not sell to them directly. Again offer to send the painting to the gallery where they can complete the sale. If you do not, and the gallery finds out that you have *stolen* their client, you will be dropped from the gallery, and word will get around quickly. It does not pay to back sell the gallery. The gallery is putting a lot of money and effort into selling your work, including advertising, shows, floor space, insurance, etc. Work with your gallery, not against it.

Review:

- The importance of a fair *Consignment Agreement*. Be sure to cover all possible eventualities.
- Follow up to insure you have the signed consignment.

Chapter 7

Setting your price

Hours and hours have been put into this painting. You researched the area, you took photographs, you created just the right composition, and of course you painted like mad to create this masterpiece. It is worth a million dollars to you, but what can you really sell it for? How do you determine the best price, especially just starting out in the art business? This is never an easy task, and can be relatively complicated, but it is not impossible.

The most difficult task you have is pricing your work. Be careful not to price your pieces too high to start, or too low. If you begin high, you may have a difficult time selling and become frustrated. If you have to lower the prices, after having them too high, this may hurt the value of the work. If a client finds out you have lowered your prices and are selling for less than they paid, you will not only lose that client, but you have single-handedly devalued your own work.

On the other hand, what if you start too low, to the point that you are practically giving your work away? You won't be doing yourself any favors. Again, what happens to the value of your paintings? You can't raise prices too quickly either.

There are no easy answers. What applies in California, may not apply in Florida, or New York. What works for a portrait artist may not work for a landscape artist. What works for you today, might not work a year from now.

Find a Mentor

Get a mentor in the art community close to where you are located. Talk to different artists, talk to galleries. The gallery where you intend to sell your work would be a good place to start. They are the front line; they know what will and will not sell; they know their market and what price they can get for the work. Seek their advice before setting your prices. If you approach a gallery for help, do so when it is their slow time. Do not walk into a crowded gallery, portfolio under your arm, at 1:00 pm on a Saturday afternoon, and expect the gallery owner to spend three hours of *their* time talking about your work, and ignoring their customers. You will never be invited back. If you want to have the gallery be your mentor, set up an appointment which is convenient to *them*. Tell them what you need their help with and ask if they would be interested in sharing their knowledge with you. If they know that you are interested in gathering information, they may be more willing to help and keep an eye on your progress.

It may be necessary to pay a consultant for assistance. Because you are a starving artist, this does not entitle you to get free advice for life. So do not impose or become a pest to those who may be able to help your career. Do your homework first. Visit shows and galleries that display your type of work. Set an appointment for ½ hour with a gallery that sells the type of work that you produce. It will not be an efficient use of your time nor theirs if you are a landscape artist and are talking to a contemporary gallery. Come prepared with photo examples of your *best* work in different sizes. Bring your bio. Have thick skin, and LISTEN to what they have to say. They are the experts in your type of art. If the gallery owner feels that your work in the 9x12 range should be selling for $200.00 ACCEPT their knowledge. Yes, you want to sell it for $2,000.00, but the work may not draw that value, yet. You can't assume that a painting hanging in a gallery for, say, $1000.00 means that your work would merit the same price. You do not know who the artist is, nor their experience and reputation in that Gallery, or their client base.

If you know a professional artist in your area of expertise, contact them, but remember do not take up a lot of their time (they have to make a living as well) and listen to what they have to say. The local professional artist will be another guide in helping price the artwork, find affordable frames and galleries selling your type of work. However, you should remember the artist may see you as competition and therefore may not give the full information you seek. Set up an appointment, keep to the time limit set, and make sure that it is convenient for the artist. Do not show up at their open studio sale, or their booth with your portfolio asking for help. The artist is there to sell their work, not to discuss yours. It is very rude to bring your artwork to their show, (where they have spent thousands of dollars to be there) spreading it out across their display table, in front of his or her customers, and expecting them to help you.

Setting Your Price

Create a working pricing scale. A 9x12 sells for say $200.00, the 8x10 goes for $150.00 etc., before adding framing costs. Granted, this may be an estimate or range. How much time have you put into research, photography, education, supplies, travel? You have a lot of factors to think about to develop your price scale. Do not determine price by the amount of hours you put into the painting. You may put 40 hours into a 9x12 and at $10.00 per hour; for example, you probably have priced yourself out of the market. You could have a 9x12 that is very impressionistic, that sells for $175, and a very detailed one that sells for $220.00. So establish a guide. You can base this on so much per square inch, but don't get too locked into the square inch table as this might not be practical when you get to certain sizes (covered in more detail later in this chapter).

Working Price Sheet *(unframed)*

8 x 10	$140.00 to $160.00
9 x 12	$175.00 to $215.00
8 x 16	$225.00 to $250.00
11 x 14	$275.00 to $325.00
12 x 16	$350.00 to $385.00

Do not try to figure your pricing structure on the number of hours that you put into the painting. Naturally some paintings will be painted quickly and you can finish them in less time than others. How would you actually calculate the hours; by the time spent at the easel? What about the time you took to research the painting, photographing the background elements, and discussing the idea with your spouse or other artists. Let's find a simpler way to calculate your pricing. Remember, when the painting is hanging in a gallery no one knows how much time you spent on it, but it is competing with the other comparable paintings.

By the Inch

Determining your pricing by the square inch is perhaps the most used method to start, if you don't have a mentor to aid you. This is not always reliable, and for some pieces you want the price to be higher than the square inch method. The idea behind the square inch pricing is pretty simple. Your 9x12 equals 108 square inches (multiply 9 by 12). Working backward, let's say you want to sell your 9x12s for $215.00; you divide your $215.00 by 108 (square inches) and arrive at the figure of $2.00. This is your guideline for the price per square inch. Now your 11x14 (154 square inches) would be $308.00 or rounded up to $310.00. Again this is just a guideline. You may want to charge $5.00 per inch; choose the number and fit it into your pricing schedule. This may be the easiest way to start pricing the work, especially if you do not have a mentor to consult. However, a painting 24x36, which would be 864 inches, might be too expensive at $5.00 per square inch, working out at $3,770.00. So adjust accordingly.

Framing Costs

Once you have determined the basic price you want to charge for your painting, you need to add the cost of framing. Let's say that the 9x12 frame costs $50.00. If you have a retail price on the painting of $200.00, and the gallery sells it for 50% commission, you walk away with only $100.00. With the $50.00 you put into the frame, your net for the painting is $50.00. Not what you expected. We suggest you take your cost of the frame and double it. In this case your $50.00 frame now is $100.00, added to the retail price of your $200.00 painting, making your new retail value $300.00. Now you will receive $150.00 in commissions, $100.00 for the painting, and $50.00 for the frame.

Recommended Retail Price

Keep the prices the same in all the galleries. So a 9x12 in New Mexico sells for $300.00 and the 9x12 in California also sells for $300.00. The gallery in New Mexico charges only a 40% commission, but the gallery in California charges 50% commission. You will make more money in New Mexico, but the buyer in California will receive the same value for the painting.

Now if you are purchasing your frames from the same company, and can pre-determine the cost of the frame, you can add that into your formula to come up with a *Recommended Retail Pricing Sheet*.

Recommended Retail Price (framed)		
Size of Painting	Frame Cost	Retail
8 x 10	$40.00	$220.00 to $240.00
9 x 12	$50.00	$275.00 to $315.00
8 x 16	$60.00	$345.00 to $370.00
11 x 14	$80.00	$435.00 to $485.00
12 x 16	$90.00	$530.00 to $565.00

As discussed in Chapter 4, framing is critical to the sale ability of the painting. Find excellent quality frames that complement the work, at the best possible price. It would not be logical to purchase a $200.00 frame for your 8x10, then have to double the cost of the frame before you add it to the recommended retail price. This would raise your $200.00 painting to $600.00, which could take it out of the price range that you need to be in.

A rule of thumb on pricing your work, is keep the same prices for 2 to 3 years; if you raise them do so only 3%-5% at first. This way you are not increasing prices every year, and pricing yourself out of the market. There is no rule that says that you must raise the price every few years. It is totally acceptable to keep the same consistent pricing for 10 years.

Now that you know the retail value of your artwork, it is time to calculate the wholesale price. Each gallery or event will have a set commission price. The commission may range from 50%-50%, to 60%-40% (you keep 60% of the retail price), or even 70%-30%. To figure the commission, multiply the retail price by 60% (for example) to determine your wholesale price. You must know what the commission structure is prior to the event, and the terms of payment. The standard in the industry is net 30 (you receive your percentage 30 days after the sale). Be sure to check that you are receiving the proper agreed upon commission in a timely manner.

Review:

- Find a mentor to help you determine pricing.
- Set the price.
- Price by the square inch.
- Framing costs.
- Recommended retail pricing.

Chapter 8

Off to the market

Shipping and Handling

Your artwork is not only important and valuable to you, but also to your clients, and needs to be handled with care. Most importantly, you want to ensure your piece arrives safely at its destination.

Whether you are sending the artwork to a gallery, show or direct to a client, the procedure is the same. The proper preparation of the documents shipped with the art is vital. You will need a large envelope (11x14) in which to place all the documents. Mark the outside of the envelope in big red letters DOCUMENTS, so the receiver does not think it is part of the packing material. We usually wrap the painting in plastic or brown paper before packing it, and we tape the *Document* envelope to the paper/plastic, before placing it in the shipping box. As discussed in Chapter 4, by now you will have put paper on the back of the painting, and created a sleeve in which to place all the documents. If the back of the frame is not papered, tape the envelope to the back of the painting.

To a Client

If you have sold the painting to a client include the following information in your *Document* envelope:
1. Bill of Sale.
2. A photo of the painting attached to the Certificate of Original Artwork.

3. *Certificate of Original Artwork.*
4. Directions on care and cleaning of your artwork.
5. Thank you letter.
6. Your bio.
7. *Fine Art Registration Card.*

Now let's take a minute and talk about each of these documents.

Bright Idea Studio
1221 South Adams
Osprey, Fl 34229

(222) 222-2222
brightideastudio@aol.com
www.BrightIdeaStudio.com

Invoice

TO: _____ Date: _____

Title	Size	Medium	Price
Vanishing Point	12x24	Acrylic	$3,500.00
		Florida State Tax (7%)	$245.00
		Shipping & Handling	$100.00
		Total Paid in Full	$3,845.00

Thank you for your purchase, and if there is anything else that we can do for you, please do not hesitate to contact us.

The artist reserves all reproduction rights, including the right to claim statutory copyright in the work. The work may not be photographed, sketched, painted, or reproduced in any manner, whatsoever without the express, written consent of the artist. All approved reproductions shall bare the following: Copyright notice by your name here ©.

Bill of Sale

The *Bill of Sale* should be printed on your letterhead, with the word *Invoice* clearly marked on the page, and should include:

1. **Purchaser; the full name, address and phone numbers.**
2. **Description of the work.**
   - I   Title, subject, medium, size and retail price
   - II   Paid in full (check, visa, MC, etc).
   - III Sales Tax (if applicable)
   - IV   Delivery Charges (if applicable)
3. **Copyright © and Reproduction statement.**

There are software packages that will generate numbered invoices, (**Quick Books** or **Artistsoftware**, for example). Determine which program works for your needs.

Note: Be careful sending out any artwork to a client that is not paid for in full. You may never see the rest of your money. If payments are being made, you may not want to send the piece until the final one has been made. Be careful of the Internet, especially in sales from overseas.

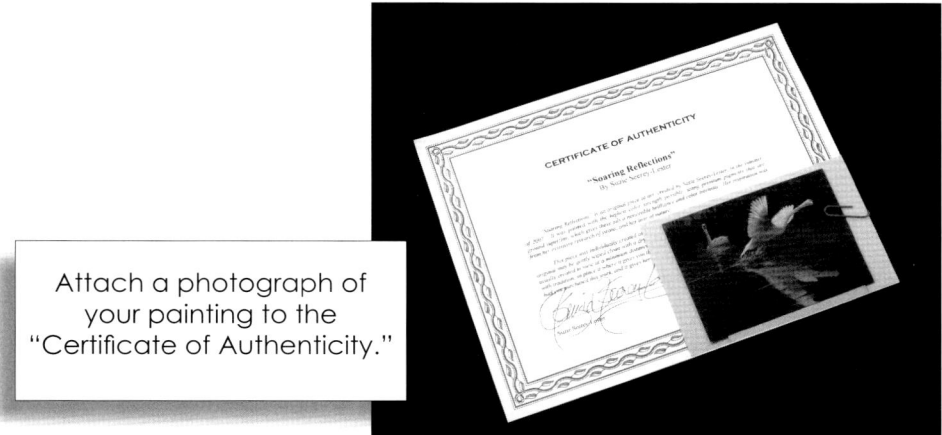

Attach a photograph of your painting to the "Certificate of Authenticity."

Photo

Attach a photo of the painting to a *Certificate of Original Artwork*. The client can keep this for their insurance records. Some software programs (**WorkingArtist**) will allow you to insert a photo of the painting onto the *Certificate of Original Artwork*.

This is an example of the "Certificate of Authenticity" to be given with every original painting.

Certificate of Original Artwork

The *Certificate of Original Artwork* can be printed on special certificate paper that you can pick up from any stationery store.

Remove this painting from the *Original Inventory List* and add it to the *Sold Inventory List*.

Care and Handling of Your Purchase

Let the customer know how to take care of this special painting, once they get it home. Create the *Care and Handling* sheet to be included with each painting. We have one for oil, and another one for acrylics.

Bright Idea Studio
1221 South Adams
Osprey, Fl 34229

(222) 222-2222
brightideastudio@aol.com
www.BrightIdeaStudio.com

Care and Handling of your Acrylic Painting

Congratulations on your purchase of Suzie Seerey-Lester's Original Art. The painting was composed and hand painted by the artist and can be expected to grow in value over the years. If you choose to sell or gift your painting, please contact the artist. (In this way collectors may be identified and records kept as the value of the piece increases.)

Your artwork was painted with the highest quality acrylic paints available on the market today. The acrylic paints that have been used are made with the maximum color strength possible, which gives these acrylics a noticeable brilliance and color intensity. If dusty or soiled, it may be gently wiped with a clean dry cloth. Refrain from using any cleaning agents, even Windex if it is under glass. If the artwork is damaged, please remember to contact the artist.

Here are two guidelines for handling your piece of fine art: Art should be displayed at eye level positioned to view from a minimum distance of 6 feet.

An example of the "Care and Handling" letter for original acrylic paintings.

Bright Idea Studio

1221 South Adams
Osprey, Fl 34229

(222) 222-2222
brightideastudio@aol.com
www.BrightIdeaStudio.com

Care and Handling of your Oil Painting

Congratulations on your purchase of Suzie Seerey-Lester's Original Art. This painting was composed and hand-painted by the artist and can be expected to grow in value over the years. If you choose to sell or gift your painting, please contact the artist. (In this way collectors may be identified and records kept as the value of the piece increases.)

Your artwork was painted with the highest quality oil paints available on the market today. The oil paints that have been used are made with the maximum color strength possible, using only pigments that are premium quality, and ground superfine, which gives these oils a noticeable brilliance and color intensity. If dusty or soiled, it may be gently wiped with a clean cloth. Refrain from using any cleaning agents, even Windex, if under glass. If the artwork is damaged, please remember to contact the artist.

Here are two guidelines for handling your piece of fine art: Art should be displayed at eye level and positioned to view from a minimum distance of 6 feet.

An example of the "Care and Handling" letter for original oil paintings.

Thank You Note

Send a thank you note with the painting, or if you choose, send it under separate cover. This client has just spent hard earned money on your masterpiece, so thank them, and they will probably purchase again in the future. This is a business where relationships build your revenues. Do not ignore it.

Your Bio

Always include your bio (which should be no more than one page). If the client wants to contact you later, it is included in his paperwork. They may also pass it on to other potential clients. Have these printed professionally, or do them yourself with special programs like **Hewlett-Packard Marketing Assistant**, which is free software that helps create fantastic brochures. There are many formats available such as tri-fold brochures, half sheets, or single sheets that will match your specific needs. Check out what they have to offer on www.hp.com. Include all events and shows in which you have participated. Include all prizes, awards received, and organizations that you belong to; such as Oil Painters of America (OPA), The Society of Animal Artists (SAA), The National Sculpture Society (NSS), and Cowboy Artists of America (CAA). By becoming a signature member of these associations, you can benefit by putting them on your bio. They may add to your reputation. They may not mean anything to your collector, because they just love the art, but they may be significant to the Director of the museum in which you are trying to get juried into a show. Some artists will use the acronym after their signatures, such as John Smith CAA, to add prestige.

Fine Art Registration Card

One final piece of information that needs to be included in the document package on the back of the paintings is the *Fine Art Registration Card*. You have seen millions of them; every time you purchase a new electronic product, a *registration* card is included. Now create a *Fine Art Registration Card*. Using Avery Post Card #8387 create your own card. On one side, enter your address, so they can send the card to you. Place a stamp on each one. On the other side your card should read: *We would appreciate it if you would please fill out this registration card so the artist can keep track of this original painting, in case of a retrospective show, damage, or loss. The increased value of your artwork may be overlooked by you and your insurance companies. Registering your original artwork will provide a provenance (the history of the painting), a* certificate of authenticity, record, and the value. And it discourages theft. Please fill in your name and address, and return this card to the Artist for "Registration". When the customer returns the card, add their information to your mailing list, keep a file on all Registrations for later use, such as provenance, and current value if ever requested by the customer.

Create a card with a place for their name, address, phone, e-mail, title of painting purchased, and date of purchase.

To the Event

If you are sending the painting to a Gallery or Show include the following in the sleeve, or an envelope on the back of the painting:

1. *Consignment Agreement* – 2 copies (Discussed in Chapter 6).
2. **Photo of the painting** attached to the inside of the crate or box, and to the *Certificate of Original Artwork* (Discussed earlier in this Chapter).
3. *Certificate of Original Artwork* (Discussed earlier in this Chapter).
4. **Directions on care and cleaning of your artwork** (Discussed earlier in this Chapter).
5. **Your Bio** (Discussed earlier in this Chapter).
6. **Painting Paragraph** Text about the painting. (Discussed in Chapter 5).

Consignment Agreement

Include two copies of the Consignment *Agreement* dealt with in Chapter Six. One is for the Gallery to keep for their records, and one is for them to sign and return to you.

Photo

You want to attach a photograph of your painting to the *Consignment Agreement* or the *Certificate of Original Artwork*. This will help the gallery identify your piece if it gets separated from the paperwork. Stick an additional photo on the inside of the crate, with your business card, so if it needs to be moved, it is moved in your crate.

Packaging

This is a critical component of your business. The painting must arrive undamaged at the location. Contact your local **UPS** or **FedEx** representatives to get their requirements for shipping glass. Package your painting as if it were a sheet of glass, then you know you have packed it correctly.

Attach the envelope with the *Consignment Agreement* to the back of the painting. Wrap the painting in a sheet of thin plastic, or brown paper. You can pick up rolls of plastic sheeting at any hardware store. Once the piece is wrapped, cut two pieces of cardboard just a little larger than the framed painting. Tape one piece to the front and one to the back then tape them together. This will keep your painting secure while it is being transported. Tape your business card to the outside of the cardboard. If the painting gets lost in shipping, when it is opened, the box will have your phone number, so you can be contacted.

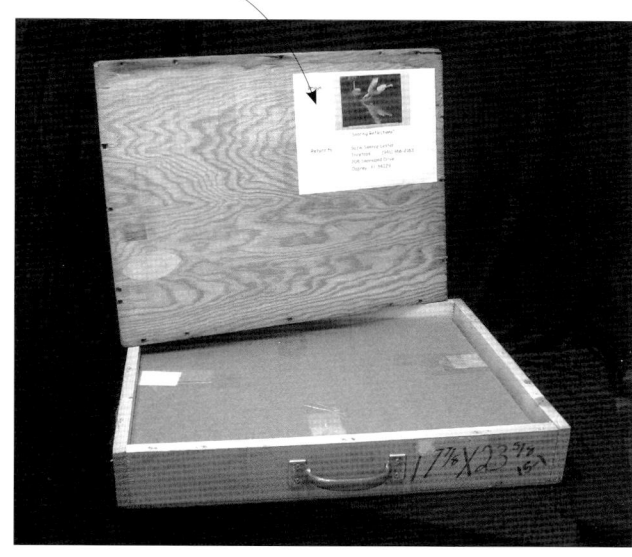

When using a crate, it is a good idea to place a photo of the painting on the inside lid with your name and return address, so the same crate will be returned to you with your painting.

Crates

Have a crate made for your painting out of wood by a local handyman. The crate should be at least 1 inch larger than your frame on all sides, and at least 2 inches deeper than your frame. Line the crate with Styrofoam or soft foam; again this will protect the painting and will prevent it from moving during shipping. Have handles on the crate for easy handling.

Using the Picture Shipper, place your painting on one foam board, place the second foam board on top. This really protects your painting for shipping.

Specialized Boxes

Another option is a **Strongbox**. These come in standard sizes, and can be ordered over the phone. The **Strongbox** has a Plexiglas shield on the front of the box, which makes it extremely strong and prevents shipping damage, and they usually have foam inside for protection.

A new version of the box type design is called a *Picture Shipper*™. This system uses an outer box, two foam panels that are attached to cardboard, and corner protectors. Simply insert the painting between the two foam panels, secure it with corner protectors or foam bumpers, then insert it in the outside box. The order information is found in Chapter 12.

The final option is cardboard boxes. If you are sending paintings out in cardboard boxes, reinforce the packaging on your piece. Wrap the plastic and cardboard covered painting in bubble wrap, then place it in the box; add additional bubble wrap to prevent it from moving.

My Painting is Done, Now What Do I Do? Simple Systems for Artists   By Suzie Seerey-Lester

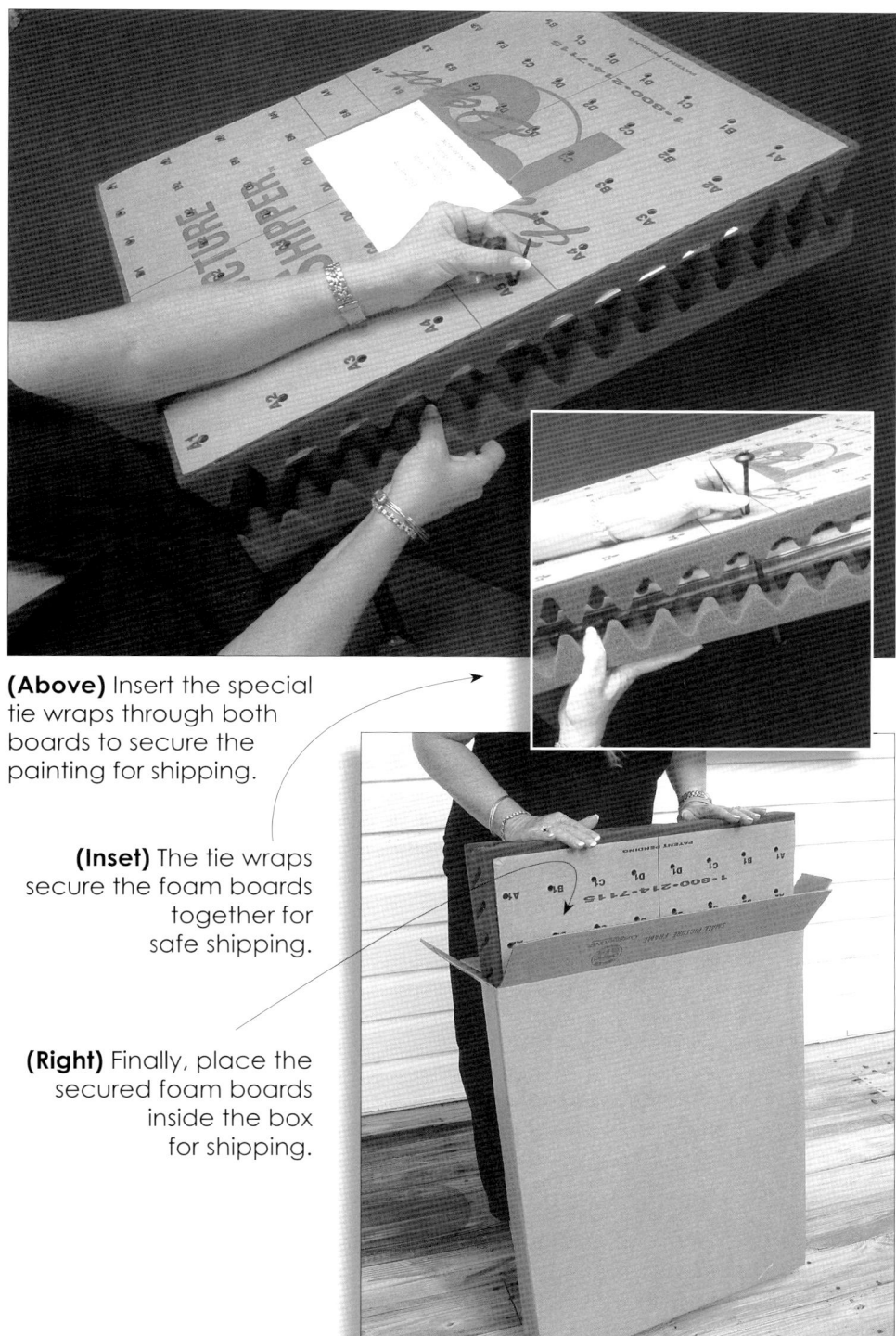

(Above) Insert the special tie wraps through both boards to secure the painting for shipping.

(Inset) The tie wraps secure the foam boards together for safe shipping.

(Right) Finally, place the secured foam boards inside the box for shipping.

Actual Shipping

Fill out the Airbill from the shipping company. Attach it to the box. In magic marker, write the Airbill Number (usually several digits on the top of the form) on the front of the box. This way if the Airbill gets separated from the box, the shipping company can locate where it needs to be delivered. Let's go one step further, and make the shipping *idiot proof*. In magic marker write: **Ship To**: Client/Gallery's full name, address, and phone number on the front of the box. **Ship From**: your name, address and phone number, in the upper left corner of the box. As a fallback you have your business card taped to the inside of the box, for further reference.

Call or e-mail your clients with the Airbill numbers so if there is a problem they can trace it on their end. Follow up the day after the painting is scheduled to arrive to insure that it has.

International Shipping

If you are shipping to a gallery or show overseas, you are required to have a *Commercial Invoice*. Discuss the value with the Gallery before you fill out this form. Depending on the country you are shipping to, they may have a VAT (value added tax) or a GST (goods and services tax); the gallery will have to pay the tax in full, upon receiving your painting. You will want to have the value of the painting showing the wholesale price, not the retail price. Also you may need a Carne, which will allow the painting to be returned to you, with no taxes being charged going or coming back into the US. Check with your International Gallery first, because they may use a different method. You will need five (5) copies of the *Commercial Invoice* attached to the Airbill when you ship the painting.

Check with the Gallery as to what they suggest the declared value of the painting to be. Some shipping companies do not want to move original paintings, and may refuse the shipment. Some shipping companies will charge you an excessive fee if they know it is original art. Some shipping companies will require you to have special insurance, which is costly. Talk to your gallery, and check on local requirements.

If your international shipment has a value in excess of $2,500.00 you are required to file an SED (Shippers Export Declaration) with the shipping company (UPS, FedEx, etc.). This document tells the US Government what is being exported where. The shipping companies will either provide you with the actual document and the instructions on filling it out, or may

Bright Idea Studio
1221 South Adams
Osprey, Fl 34229

(222) 222-2222
brightideastudio@aol.com
www.BrightIdeaStudio.com

Commercial Invoice

Consignee: _____   Date: _____

The Gallery _____

Street _____   Phone: _____

City _____

Country _____

Qnty	Description of Goods	Value
1	WC# 07/01 Reflections of Nature	$3500.00
	Total	$3500.00

These commodities were exported from the United States in accordance with the export administration regulations. Diversion contrary to US Law prohibited.

I hereby certify that the information on this invoice is true and correct and that the contents of this shipment are as stated above. I do hereby authorize Fed X (or UPS, etc.) to execute any additional documents necessary for the export of merchandise described herein on my behalf.

Signature: _____
Name: *Your name here* _____
Title: _____

allow you to fill it out electronically. You will need your EIN# (if you are Incorporated, you are assigned one) or you can use your social security number. Ask the shipping company to give you the Schedule B Number (The Schedule B Number is a code assigned to all products that are exported from the United States, so the government can keep track of everything that is exported) for *display material* or *graphics*; this is required on the SED. Attach the SED with the five Commercial Invoices to the Airbill.

Review:

Prepare Your Paperwork for a Client with:
- Bill of Sale.
- Photo of painting.
- Certificate of Original Artwork.
- Care and Handling letter.
- Thank you letter.
- Your Bio and literature.

Prepare Your Paperwork for a Gallery or Show:
- Consignment Agreement – 2 copies.
- Photo of painting.
- Certificate of Original Artwork.
- Care and Handling letter.
- Your Bio and Literature.
- Paragraph about the painting.

Packaging:
- Wrap the painting in plastic sheet.
- Tape cardboard to front and back.
- Wrap in bubble wrap if necessary.
- Place in foam-lined crate.

Shipping:
- Fill out the Airbill.
- Write the Airbill number on the crate.
- Write the Ship To information on the crate.
- Write the Ship From information on the crate.

International Shipping:
- Five copies of the Commercial Invoice attached to the Airbill.
- SED if value exceeds $2500.00 attached to the Airbill.

Chapter 9

The exhibition

The Seven P's
(Prior Preparation Prevents any Possibility of Piss Poor Performance)

You have been accepted into a show, now what do you do? The show is next month, and you need to get organized, set up, ready to go to the show. You want to be well prepared, and efficient, so you are not spending all day figuring out where the paintings will be placed.

Show Inventory List

You have already completed the *Original Information Sheet*, so you know the painting has been photographed (prints and slides), varnished; and the three labels (title label, copyright label and notice label) are on the back, the painting is framed with the nameplate attached. You have now decided which paintings you will have on display. The next step is to create the *Show Inventory List* for easy reference during the event.

The *Show Inventory List* will be made up of the titles, sizes, medium and retail price of your paintings. Use this to check the paintings in and out of the studio, and the show. An example of a *Show Inventory List* is on the next page.

After you have finished the *Show Inventory List*, now package the paintings. If you are shipping them, note the box number, i.e. #3, # 5, etc. next to the title of the painting, on the *Show Inventory List*. If you are driving them locally, use the box system, described on page 104 to help you stay organized.

ABC Gallery Summer Show - July 7, 2007

Bright Idea Studio
1221 South Adams
Osprey, Fl 34229

	WC#	Title	Size	Medium	Retail
1	07/08	Dark Reflections	9x12	Oil	$ 1,000.00
2	06/51	Early Risers	9x12	Acrylic	$ 1,500.00
3	07/10	Evening Sojourn	15x30	Oil	$ 4,000.00
4	06/49	Great White Hunter	8x10	Acrylic	$ 800.00
5	07/03	Morning Preen	12x9	Acrylic	$ 1,500.00
6	07/02	Morning Stroll	8x16	Oil	$ 3,000.00
7	07/01	Reflections of Nature	12x24	Acrylic	$ 3,500.00
8	07/07	Silent Stalker	12x24	Oil	$ 3,500.00
9	07/06	Sitting on a Sandbar	8x16	Oil	$ 3,000.00
10	07/05	Southern Nights	8x10	Acrylic	$ 800.00
11	07/11	Vanishing Point	12x24	Acrylic	$ 3,500.00
12	05/23	Winter Water	9x12	Oil	$ 1,500.00

Box System

Make several boxes out of cardboard slightly larger than the width of the frames, and wide enough to hold 3 to 5 paintings each. These do not have to be fancy. You can cut a handle and not make a lid. Each box will have it's own letter, i.e. A, B, C, etc. As you place a painting into a box, write the box number next to the painting on the *Show List*. This check system works in two ways; you know the piece has been packed, and in which box. Now pack the boxes into your vehicle at your leisure. Using this system the paintings are protected, they don't slide around, and the boxes take up much less space than stacking the paintings. You can easily carry 3-5 paintings at once into the show using the boxes and place them under the panel where they are to be hung. It is just as easy to break down the show, placing each painting into a box to be moved out after the show. We also use a garden cart to move the boxes in and out of the show. It is easier and quicker than hand carrying them.

Using the box system, you can easily move several paintings at a time, quickly and easily with a garden cart.

Booth Plan

The event will let you know in advance the amount of space that is allocated to your artwork and the configuration. You know how many paintings will be displayed and their sizes, so now you can create the *Booth Plan*. Let's say for example you will have five panels for your booth. The standard panel is 8'x4'; the show will let you know if it is not a standard size. Draw out a template of the booth; keep extra copies as spares to modify the booth again, if necessary. Using a pencil, draw in the paintings to scale on the panels in your template. You can easily layout your booth, change it; modify it on paper before arriving at the show. At the show, pull out the *Booth Plan*, and hang your booth according to the plan. Fast, easy and simple.

When designing the *Booth Plan*, have the subject of the paintings pointed into the booth. For example, if you have a crow flying left, this piece should be hung on the right side panel. All subjects should face the same direction on the panel, with the outside panels having the subjects looking/moving/ pointing into the booth. Hang the most important (largest) piece in the center of the booth and your eye-catching pieces on the outside panel to bring people into the booth. A lot of this placement will depend on the booth layout and location at the show.

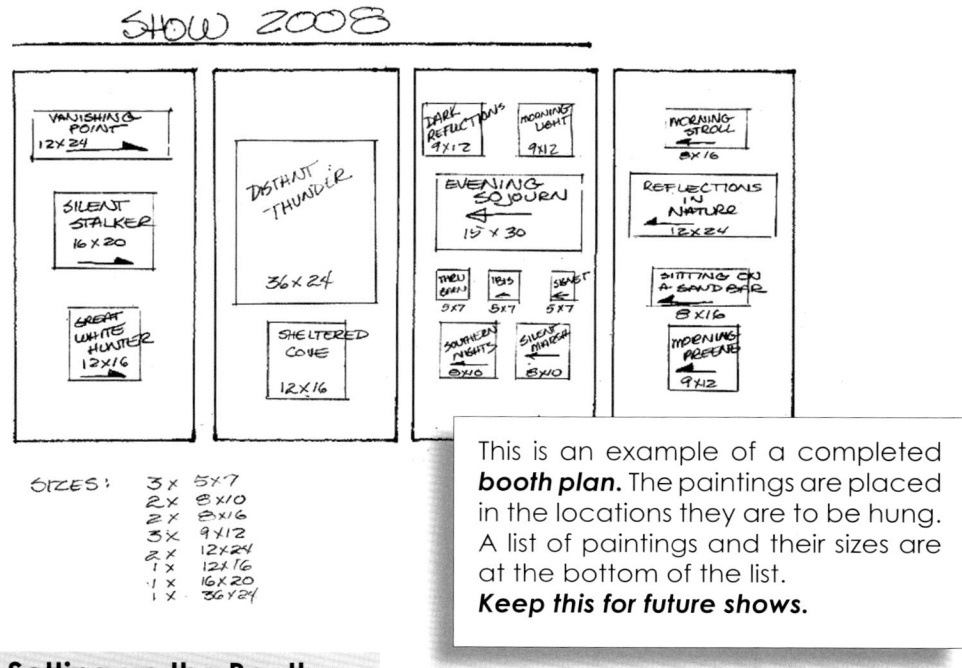

This is an example of a completed **booth plan.** The paintings are placed in the locations they are to be hung. A list of paintings and their sizes are at the bottom of the list.
Keep this for future shows.

Setting up the Booth

Bring all the hardware that you will need for the booth, i.e. S-hooks, C-hooks, peg board hooks, curtain pins, Velcro, Blue Tack, etc. Use only what is accepted by the show management. At one show people were stapling things to the pegboard without the permission of the show. It ruined the pegboard, and some of the staples went thru the board and damaged artwork on the other side. When in doubt, ask before you take any action. Some shows want you to decorate your booth. One of our friends used to create an astonishing paper cave around his booth, which drew people in, and helped the sales. Other booths have cozy furniture, flowers, some decorated with fabric. All very uniquely designed to make the clients remember the artists. Not all shows allow creativity. Some will only allow the painting and price cards. Some will have tables, others will not. Please follow the rules of the show. All this information will be written in the show information package that you receive. If it is not, please call the show promoters prior to arriving with your questions.

My Painting is Done, Now What Do I Do? Simple Systems for Artists   By Suzie Seerey-Lester

Sometimes John and I have booths next to each other, as well as a TV in one booth, playing our DVD's.

Painting in your booth can create interest, and it gives you an easy opportunity to start a conversation with a buyer that may lead to a sale.

My Painting is Done, Now What Do I Do? Simple Systems for Artists   By Suzie Seerey-Lester

Do not over crowd your booth. Make it interesting and inviting for people to come in and get a closer look.

If you have large pieces that will not fit on the panels, place them on easels inside the booth.

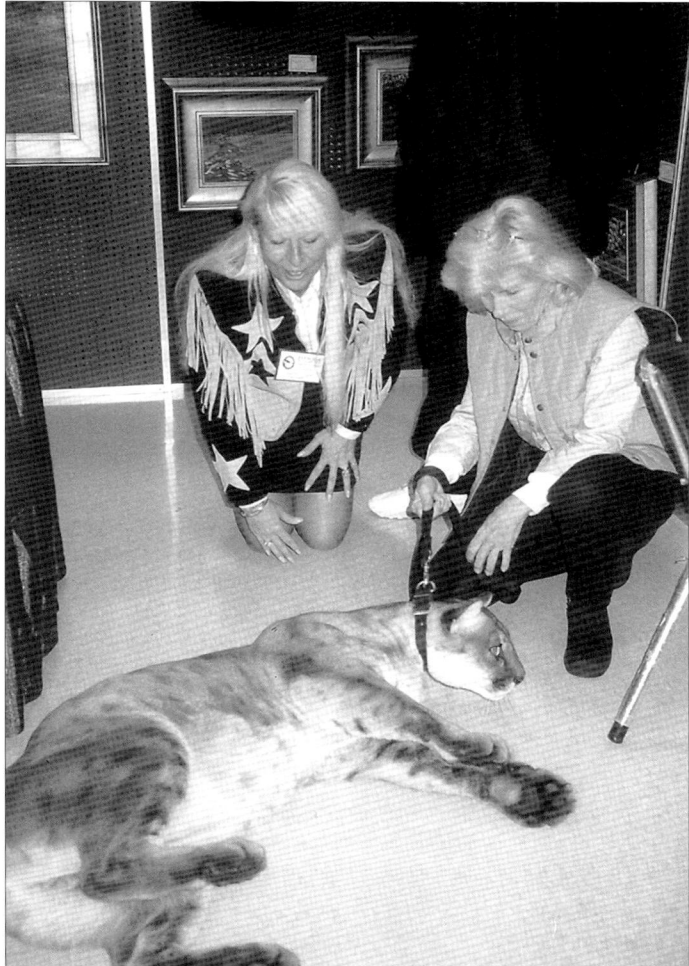

Here is a Florida Panther that joined us in the booth. This draws lots of attention and brings people into your area.

Have your business cards and biography available to hand out to clients that ask for them. If you have a pile of business cards and brochures sitting on a table, the *paper collectors* (usually 5 year old kids) will come by and scoop up your expensive paperwork. Keep one or two out, keep the rest at easy access.

Bring breath mints. Enough said. Have bottled water in the booth, and keep it out of the way of the customers.

Getting Psyched for a Show

Shows are EXCITING! There is lots of activity going on, with everyone getting ready for the show. Be realistic about your goals. Go into a show with the attitude that if you don't sell anything, that is ok because it is a learning experience, and you get to hang out with other artists you haven't seen for a while, and have fun. Some artists get depressed if they don't sell in the first day. So they sit in the corner, arms crossed, legs crossed; it shows that they are unhappy. They get angry, and of course it shows even more, and people don't want to buy from them. You must psych yourself up for the show. Be happy, smile at everyone that comes into your booth. It is contagious. People want to purchase from happy artists. It makes them feel good, and it will make you feel good as well. Yes your feet hurt, you have been insulted a 1000 times, but keep smiling, and you will sell!

Red Dots

One key ingredient for any booth is RED DOTS. Bring your own supply of self-adhesive red dots that you purchase from any stationery store. When you sell a painting, place a red dot on the price card. If the customer takes the artwork with them, take the price card with the red dot and stick it to the side of the booth. As more and more pieces are sold, add the price cards with the red dots underneath the first sold card. The red dots can start a buying frenzy. This shows buyers that you are selling lots of pieces, and they better purchase now, before everything is gone. It is also a fun competition between artists, to see who is selling the most artwork. On occasions, during a slow show, we will place a red dot on an unsold painting to create interest, and start a buying trend. Place this red dot on a piece that you think may not sell, because you don't want to lose the sale.

Different Types of Shows

There are all types of shows with which you can become involved. Be creative, find a niche for your type of artwork.

Not for Profit Shows

This may be a good way to get your foot in the door and to start selling your work. Select a charity in your area that has a yearly fund-raiser. Several that we are involved with are: Big Brothers, Big Sisters, The Loveland Center, The Audubon Society, YMCA, MS, MD, and several Cancer organizations. Local Animal shelters or organizations are always in need of funds. Rotary, and other service organizations, are other options. The local Hospitals may also have annual fund raisers. Also look into your local chapters of Ducks Unlimited (DU), Quail Unlimited (QU), Safari Club International (SCI), Elk Federation, etc. Join or get involved with some of these organizations. You may be able to give presentations about your artwork (select a theme, environmental, architecture, etc., that represents your artwork and build talks around the paintings.) When the organizations have their yearly fund-raiser, donate a print or allow an original to be auctioned. Talk with the organizers to insure that you receive your reserve (discussed in the Auction Section, page 126) and that any funds raised over your reserve are donated to the charity. The customer receives a tax deduction because they write a check to i.e., *Big Brothers*, not to you. The charity receives money, and you get publicity. Be sure to write a *Press Release* regarding your donation and send it out to all the local papers. You will soon have a name in your local area for working with charities. This may lead to purchases down the road.

Other Types of Shows

There are many famous artists that the *person next door* instantly recognizes for their art. Bev Doolittle for her camouflage art; Kinkade, the *Painter of Light*; and who hasn't seen one of the world's great whales painted on the side of a bank building or water tank, thanks to Wyland? As a new artist, or as a professional artist, you need to create an *identity*. What or how you paint, needs to be easily recognized at a glance.

Find venues that are associated with your artwork. One of our good friends is a wonderful marine artist, painting fish, and marine life. He attends the large boat shows in Florida and sells his paintings. There is a lot of money in boats, and boaters may need a small painting for their yacht or home. The artist is well known at these shows, with customers returning year after year to purchase his new work. Home Improvement Shows offer another venue, with thousands of people attending. Paint in your booth to attract more attention. Flower Shows are a great venue for landscape artists, or those who specialize in flora. Garden Shows are also quite successful. Some wineries are interested in having art shows during their wine tasting venues, and may even have music playing to add to the event. These organizations will bring in people. You need to have unique pieces available to sell at these settings. Equestrian events represent lots of money. If you paint horses and related subjects, set up at Polo Matches, Horse Shows, high-end Rodeos. Go where the money is, make yourself unique, and create a forte that is in high demand.

Be creative, there may be other opportunities to have Open Studio Sales. In our area, at Christmas time, a local ladies charity holds a *Christmas Walk of Homes*. These are usually large mansions, decorated to the hilt, everyone is curious about what the homes look like on the inside. The *Walk of Homes* is very popular. There is usually lots of local publicity, prior to the event, and we make sure there is information about our studio event. It is run just like the Open Studio as described in Chapter 5, but the charity collects all the money, including an entry fee. The charity will pay us a commission (between 60%-80% depending on the charity). They advertise, they promote your studio/home, they do all the paperwork, including insurance. They will have docents answering questions, taking the pressure off you. They collect the tax, and pay that as well. All customers receive a tax write off.

Get involved with the local art organizations. We are involved with several including the **Fine Art Society of Sarasota, The Venice Art Center**, to name a few. Once a year these organizations develop a Studio Tour visiting local artists' studios. Again, this is a form of fund raising for these groups. They do all the advertising, print beautiful brochures, maps and information on each artist. This is a major event every year. Most organizations rotate artists, so make the most of the event. Again, they will have docents provide information, collect money, and pay you a commission. It is always fun to paint during these events, because people are interested in what *real artists* create. It is just another opportunity to close a sale.

Suzie discussing one of her paintings with interested visitors to her booth.

Build a Relationship with your Clients

To increase your sales potential, you need to keep great records and build a relationship with all your clients. Every time a painting is sold, record who purchased the piece in your *Sold Inventory List*. Keep a folder on each client, including their name, address, phone number, e-mail, birthday, types of subjects in which they are interested, their price range, and family names (wives, husbands, kids). Keep in touch with clients by sending out VIP packages to them once a quarter, or a newsletter. If you know their birthdays, send a card. Send Christmas/Holiday cards, using one of your own images. Remember that they may have a home in Crystal River, and when you have a painting that may suit them, send them a photo. Do not be overbearing with these clients, because they will disappear quickly. Do not pressure them to constantly purchase. Do not send paintings to them on spec without their permission. Keep the dialog friendly, and professional at all times. The more information that you can gather in a normal conversation, the better the relationship you can build for years to come.

Assembling Your Own Booth (Tents)

When selling at outdoor shows you must realize that you have no control over where you will be placed or what the weather will be like, so you must prepare for everything. The spaces are usually 10'x10'. It could be on the North side one year, and the South side the next. In the sun one time, then in the shade another time. Rain, wind, hot one day, and freezing the next. So you realize the placement can't be controlled nor can the environment. The most important criteria is a high quality booth. It must be weather proof, waterproof, and wind proof and should be made of high quality waterproof vinyl, with four fully zippered sidewalls, and if possible, heat and wind vents in the top. The frame should be all steel to make it sturdy. The inexpensive *pop up* tents are not recommended. Be prepared for all types of weather when selling at outdoor shows. The tent is your security blanket for your valuable artwork. We recommend **CraftHut Tents**. You can find them at www.flourish.com. They also have Mesh Panel Display walls that are excellent. To make your booth more professional, cover your mesh or wire panels with a neutral color cloth (black or gray). Jersey, and stretch materials work well. Select a fabric that will not show holes from the drapery hooks that you use to hang the paintings. This gives a finished look to the booth; you won't be able to see through the panel, and it sets your paintings on a viewing area that is complementary to the paintings.

Have a dolly or a garden wagon (discussed earlier in this chapter) ready to move all your artwork into the tent. This will save you lots of headaches because you usually can not park close to the booth, and you may have to walk a few blocks back and forth between the car and the booth.

Set up as early as you can. The tent comes first. Include weights on all four corners to add stability against wind. In some locations, the organizers will allow you to anchor (nail) the tent into the ground. Be sure to check. If you are on grass, stake all four corners and add weights as well. After the tent is up and solid, build your panels. Attach the panel to the frame of the tent in several locations. We can recommend the *Mesh Panel Display* walls by *Flourish Co* **(www.flourish.com)** or *Pro Panels* at **www.propanels.com**, the latter being heavy, but more stable.

Use a booth plan to set up your tent. The booth plan is discussed earlier in this chapter. You can mix prints with originals, or have originals in one location, framed prints in another. Some people will set up the panels at home, hang the show, and mark on the booth plan where they have placed everything.

A well set up tent is easy to enter and walk around. Paintings on easels outside the tent are inviting to people, as long as it does not effect your neighbor.

Outdoor show with all the tents lined up. Make your tent different and inviting to bring people in to see your work.

My Painting is Done, Now What Do I Do? Simple Systems for Artists   By Suzie Seerey-Lester

"Hey Dad, this has superb brushwork, an almost classic composition, and an ethereal use of light. It reminds me of early Renaissance–I love it!"

Keep the originals high (lots of kids like to touch paintings that are low to the ground). Keep all prints out of the sun; if the print is in shrink-wrap it will wrinkle, if the print (or original) is under glass, the sun will cause condensation and will ruin the piece. If you are forced to place something in the sun, it should be an original oil or acrylic, which will not be damaged by the sun for a short period of time. With the mesh panels you can use drapery hooks to hang the paintings and prints; use two per painting to insure the image is straight.

Keep the opening of the tent clear so people feel comfortable getting in and out of the small space. If you crowd the opening with print bins, browsers, tables, and chairs, people will feel claustrophobic and may not even stick their heads in your booth. Make every inch count. If you are going to stand (or sit in a *director's* chair) do so at the back of the booth. If you sit outside the booth, it is like you are guarding the space; again, this may stop people from entering. Make your tent inviting. Keep it as open as possible. Most of the panel manufacturers make podiums, which are desks with storage areas for your credit card machine, sales book, and any additional paper work you may need. They have print boxes that match the panels, or you can make print boxes for standard size prints. Make your booth work for you. Keep it clean and neat, it will look larger, and more inviting.

Have a mobile wireless credit card machine. These are easily available from your credit card provider, as discussed in Chapter 5. If you don't take credit/debit cards you will not make many sales. Have the customer fill out their information in your two part sales book, (discussed in Chapter 5) while you run the credit card. Be sure to get the phone number, e-mail, and address, on all sales. You can add all the names and addresses from your sales book to mailing lists and keep your customers informed about your next show.

Have lots of little things for sale with a value of $20.00 or less. They can be small matted images, a pack of note cards, etc. These are your bread and butter and help pay for your booth space. Make sure you have lots of change on hand. Shrink-wrap all your prints onto foam core, or use crystal clear envelopes **(www.clearbags.com)** to package your images. These clear bags come in different sizes, and are great for standard sized matted prints.

Be ready for everything. Bring extra print bins in different sizes to fit where you can inside the tent. Bring extra originals; so as you sell one, replace it with another piece. Have price tag descriptions next to each piece, clearly marked as an original or a print, with the retail price. Have plastic bags (can be purchased on a roll for easy storage) to wrap your customer's purchase when they leave your booth.

At night, remove all your artwork from the booth. Outdoor shows usually have security, but it is worth the extra 30 minutes to move your originals out, rather than have them stolen. The shows are usually not responsible for loss or damage. Better to be safe than sorry.

Apply to the shows early and chose your shows wisely. If you are selling fine art, apply to those shows, and not craft shows. It is very difficult to sell a $5,000.00 painting at an outdoor show, when the lady in the next booth is selling jams she made in her kitchen for $2.50.

Photo Book

Have your *Photo Album* (Discussed in Chapter 5) available for all the clients to see. They can see other examples of your work, and may find something they would like to commission. This is also a wonderful way to start a conversation with potential clients.

Price Cards

You have hung your booth, and now it is time to hang the price cards. Prior to going to the show, make pre printed price cards using business card stock, purchased at the local office supply store. This will give your booth a uniform and professional touch. They come in many colors and styles. Your tags should have the following information: Title (in largest type) below that, your name, the next line will be the medium and size, and the final line will be the price.

Price Tag:

> *Reflections in Nature*
> By Suzie Seerey-Lester
> 12x24 Acrylic
> $3,500.00

Some shows will provide you with price cards, usually printed with their logo, and a standard size for everyone. If they provide them, use them. Standardizing the pricing cards throughout the show makes it easy for the clients. Use clear labels to type the information then place them on the *show* cards; it will look more professional than hand writing the cards. One way of doing this is to use transparent labels, which can be applied to the price cards, supplied by the show organizers.

John in his theme booth. Note he has a painting paragraph with the photo mounted on foam core. These are silent salesmen telling the story of your painting. The smaller cards are the price cards.

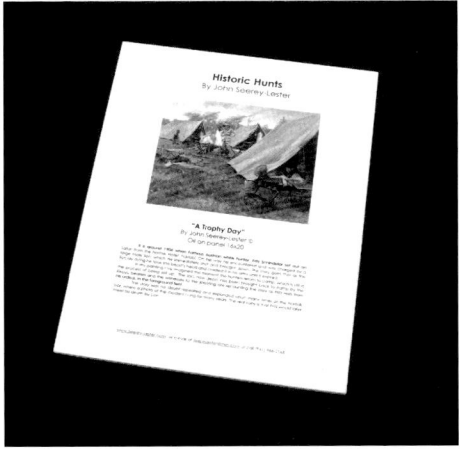

Here is an example of a painting paragraph with the photo mounted on foam core. This can be done for every painting, and placed next to it as a conversation piece.

Painting Paragraph

As we discussed in Chapter 6, you want to have a paragraph describing the painting; just a short note typed up as a sales aid. You can mount your *Painting Paragraph* on mat board and place it next to the painting. This is a silent salesman for you. People can come in and easily read the paragraph about the painting. It may help nudge them over the edge into the sale of your painting. Anything that you can use to help sell the painting (with the blessing of the show organizer), the better.

Leaving the booth

If you have to leave the booth for lunch (NEVER eat in the booth), or a bathroom break, ask the artist next to you to cover your booth, and do the same for them. Do not ask someone else to cover your booth for too long. If you are gone frequently or for excessive periods of time, it shows that you don't want to be there and you really don't care about sales. During slow periods walk around and talk to your neighbor artists, but stay within sight and earshot of your booth, in case someone comes in.

Sales

How potential buyers perceive you will assist your sales. If you are happy, smiling, up beat and open to people entering the booth, you are more likely to make a sale. If you sit in the corner of the booth, reading a book, arms and legs crossed, never looking up or speaking to potential buyers, you are telling them you don't want to talk to them, let alone sell them one of your paintings. When someone enters your booth, ask him or her questions they can only answer in a positive way. For example; Are you enjoying the show? What is your favorite animal? My favorite line is; Have you fallen in love yet? Meaning falling in love with one of the paintings. This usually breaks the ice and makes them laugh. Come up with your own; don't steal mine! Some people will run away if you approach them, because they think you are going to do a hard sell on them. Watch their body language, if they point at your piece, come back to look at it again, stare at it for hours, drool over it, or have a discussion with someone else about one of your paintings, this is a good sign to approach them, and offer some information about the piece. Don't be overbearing – remember good art sells itself and it comes down to personal taste. There is a buyer out there for every painting.

Another method of engaging conversation is to comment on what they are wearing; *That blue looks wonderful on you. What a fascinating necklace you have. It looks stunning on you.* Again use anything non-threatening to get them to connect with you. If they like the color blue, take them over to your painting that has blue in it and point to the Painting Paragraph, or better yet, tell a story about the painting. You want them to bond with you. People love to talk about themselves, so let them. The more they talk to you, the better chance of making a sale.

Another way to talk to clients is to tell them about the booth. For example, *The paintings on this panel are all Plein Air, which means that we painted them in the field, during a snowstorm. The paintings on the side are all studio paintings, created from my travels in the field.* You could be showing them a painting of a tiger in a zoo, but you saw it during your research, and they are always interested in hearing stories from the artist. Pay attention to which paintings they are looking at more than others and tell them something specific about that piece or similar pieces.

Know when to shut up. If a client is contemplating a painting, give them some space. People can tell when you are desperate, so don't be hopeless; be engaging, fun, and pleasant. Shut up and back off. If they need further encouragement, you will know. Fine art cannot be a hard sell. Fine art is an emotional sale; people have to connect with your artwork. If you have something in your painting that *speaks* to them, they are more likely to

purchase it. If you get your gun out and place it on the table and ask them to make a decision, you will not encourage them to buy. Instead all you will see is their back running away as fast as possible. Keep smiling even though they don't buy, thank them for their time. They may buy in the future, and they may return to your booth later during the show.

You can't tell a potential buyer by what they are wearing. Whether they are dripping in diamonds, or wearing shorts and a T-shirt, you just don't know who the buyers are. Be nice to everyone. Spend as much time with the guy in the aloha shirt as the one in the expensive silk suit. Both types will appreciate it and remember that you cared enough to spend time with them.

Once a client has selected one of your paintings, walk them through the sales process. Take them over to the sales table, or get the Show's appointed sales person. Walk with the buyer and talk to them, until the sale is final. Thank them.

Send them a thank you note when you get home. This is very important. Also put them on your mailing list and/or client list.

A word of warning. At the end of the show, when everyone is packing up, some clients will circulate and try to purchase paintings at a discount – so you don't have to pack it up and take them home. Do Not Discount your work. Some clients will try to get around paying the show their percentage.

For example; *I will meet you in the parking lot and give you cash for your painting, provided you give me a 40% discount.* This is bad news and should be reported to the show management. Do not burn your bridges with the show by back selling. No matter how desperate you feel, it will harm you in the long run, and it will get back to the show management. Other clients will contact you days or weeks after the show, again wanting to purchase the work, at a discount. Do not discount. Accept the full amount and send the show a commission check. When you do this, the show management will see that you are ethical and are willing to follow the rules. It is a sure way to get invited back next year. When in doubt ask yourself, what is the ethical way to proceed.

Show Check List

We use a *Show Check List* while preparing for the show and loading our vehicle to insure that everything that we need for the show is in the booth on opening night. Shown on the next page is our checklist which you will want to modify to fit your actual needs. We have been using this list for years, modifying it as we need. We go out Plein Air Painting everywhere, including early mornings before the show opens. This is another way to attract attention in your booth, having a painting that is wet because you just finished it at 6:00 am, painting a local scene outside in the freezing cold. Anything to sell a painting!

Check In	Check Out	Bright Idea Studio
		1221 South Adams
		Osprey, Fl 34229
		Show Check List
Check In	Check Out	Item
		Biography Brochures
		Blue Tack (for price tag, paragraphs, etc)
		Book Holders
		Books (about or featuring the artist)
		Booth Backdrop
		Box System (numbered boxes for paintings)
		Brochure Holders
		Brochures on Paintings, DVDs, Books, etc.
		Browser for prints or unframed originals
		Business Cards
		Business Card Holder
		Calculator
		Computer, Printer, Cables
		Credit Card Machine (Outdoor shows)
		Digital Camera, battery charger, etc
		Double Sided Tape
		Frame Assembly Equipment
		Framed Photo of Artist
		Framed Prints
		Guest Book
		Handy-wipes
		Magic Marker
		Mapquest
		Masking Tape
		Name Signs
		New Paintings on CD
		Original Inventory List (Price, size, etc)
		Painting Paragraphs
		Paintings
		Pegboard clips, s hooks, etc.,
		Photo Album of Current Pieces
		Plan of Booth
		Price Cards
		Prints

Show Inventory List
Signing Pens
Sun Glasses
Swiffer to clean frames & paintings
Table Easels
Tool Box
Unframed originals
Walkie Talkies
Wire Clippers

**Should you Choose to Paint
at or during the Show:**

Acrylic Brushes
Acrylic Paints
Backpacks
Binoculars
Bug Spray
Cooler and Cold Drinks (water, soda)
Easels
Extra Frames for Plein Air done during show
Odorless Mineral Spirits
Oil Brushes
Oil Paints
Paint Box - Open Box M
Panels, Canvas, Boards
Paper Palette
Paper Towels
Seperator Box (for wet paintings)
Sketch Books
Sting Ease
Turps Pots
Walking Stick (Mall Stick)
Water for Acrylics
Water Pots
Watercolor kit
Watercolor post cards

Show Breakdown

Never start taking paintings off the wall prior to the designated breakdown time. If the breakdown time is 5:00 pm on Sunday, do not start at 4:45 pm. Wait until the show is officially over. You may have that last minute buyer running into your booth to grab the piece that they just can't live without. The breakdown is always easier and faster than the setup. Once again be considerate of your neighbor: don't leave packing material where others have to walk. Don't move their artwork to the exit. Take each painting down and put it back into the *painting box*. When your booth is totally broken down, then go get your car so others can pack their vehicles as well. Collect all your pegboard clips; pull off all the old price cards. Leave your booth as clean as it was when you arrived for the set-up. Thank the show management for all their assistance in making the show successful. Always send a written thank you note when you return home.

Just a quick note, don't brag about your sales. Some artists will have wonderful shows, others may be struggling. One time you may be the artist struggling, and would feel more comfortable if the successful artists were gracious about their sales. Treat others like you want to be treated and you will always succeed.

Auctions

On occasion you may be asked to participate in an auction. These can be an excellent public relations exercise for you. This is a way to get your name out in the community, and find potential future buyers. You could be asked to donate your piece totally, or a percentage of the value, depending on your agreement. You will need a letter for the IRS to cover your donation (full or the percentage).

Auctions are designed to sell your piece to a buyer so they can either raise funds for a charity, or to make money. When you put a piece in the auction you want to list the retail price, for example the painting is valued at $2,000.00, and the reserve price, in this example: $1,500.00. The reserve is the lowest value that the auctioneer can accept for your panting. If you do not have a reserve, your painting may sell for a lot less than you expected. After the sale, depending on your agreement with the auction house, the artist usually receives 50% to 70% of the selling price. On your consignment invoice, you must list retail and reserve prices. Talk to the auctioneer or the person running the auction to make sure they understand your reserve price. A recent example was a $15,000.00 retail value painting was sold for $2,500.00 because there was no reserve placed on the piece. The artist received only $1250.00 for the $15,000.00 painting. On a happier note, you may receive a much higher price; for example, a $15,000.00 painting sold for $25,000.00, the artist received $12,500.00. Almost the full retail price!

It is important that you realize that the selling price at an auction can't really affect your usual market price. If a 24"x36" $15,000.00 painting sold for $2500.00, this does not mean all your 24"x36" paintings are worth this price. We know some artists who have received higher than normal prices at auctions, then went on to try and sell all their work at the higher rate and failed miserably. In the end they had to reduce their retail prices and

their market never fully recovered. A savvy collector will see what your work fetched at auction and consider themselves to be getting a good deal buying your work at the regular retail price. They are getting a good deal of course, because your work can sell for more and will probably appreciate in value.

Review:

- Show Inventory.
- Box System.
- Booth Plan.
- Setting up the Booth.
- Photo Album.
- Price Cards.
- Painting Paragraph.
- Leaving the Booth.
- Sales.
- Show Check List.
- Show Breakdown.
- Send Thank You Cards.
- Auctions.

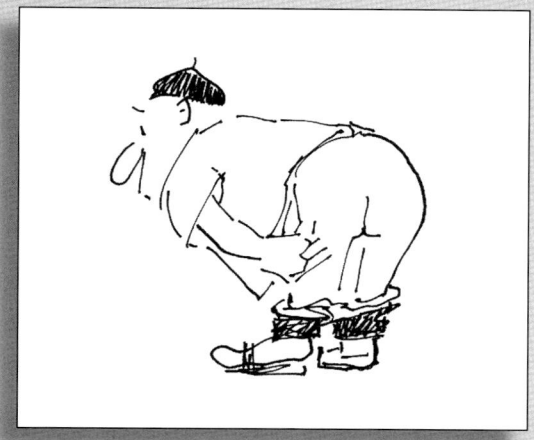

Chapter 10

Artist etiquette

Don't burn your bridges before you start your career

An entire book should be written on artist etiquette, and should be given to all new artists. Yes, these are all the things Mom taught you growing up, that you probably forgot years ago. Time to pull them out of the closet.

New artists should visit as many art shows as possible and learn as much as you can *by observing*. See how the booths are set up, see the type of frames they are using. What is their pricing structure like? What do their brochures talk about? What do their business cards look like? What types of paintings are selling the best in the show? Is it the size, price range, or subject matter? This is the best way to learn about the art business, and whether you would be interested in doing a particular type of show. Visit open-air shows, visit fine art shows, visit gallery shows, visit shows in libraries, museums, or at the local coffee shop. Go to shows that sell just wildlife, landscapes, sculptures, contemporary artwork, western, photography, modern; see how they all differ, and which ones you like the best. Frequently the local art center will put on shows. Try to attend them. Your local Fine Art Society may have studio walks where you get to see different artists at work. Go. It will be well worth your time. Artists will love to talk to you, but please limit questions to just a few, and be respectful of the artist's selling time. If you are truly interested in becoming a professional artist, you must do your homework first.

The golden rule should be: *never burn your bridges*. The way you behave at an event will have a great deal of impact on how you are perceived by other artists, the show organizers and the clients. Your behavior can have more influence on sales than the artwork. This can happen in several different ways. Remember the artist who sent enormous files unsolicited to the gallery, tying up the gallery's computer for half the day. That is a prime example of burning bridges. That artist will never be able to set foot in that gallery, and probably all the nearby galleries as well. Word gets around quickly, especially if it is negative. If you show up late, complain about the size of your booth, leave early, break down early, moan and whine about everything, chances are pretty good that you may not sell anything, and probably will not be asked back to the show. No one wants to hang around someone negative, let alone help him or her, and no one wants to buy from pessimistic artists.

DO NOT bring your portfolio/artwork/photos of your artwork into another artist's booth. This is NEVER appropriate. Do not bring your work into a place where someone else is selling his or her artwork. It doesn't matter if it is a gallery, a booth show, an open house, or a studio sale. Don't even ask if you can show your work to another artist, while they are working. You are putting them in a position where they have to say yes, and it is still inappropriate. If you are asking for a critique, make an appointment after the show hours, outside of the show area, for example in your hotel lobby, in the restaurant, or bar. Never during the show nor in someone else's booth. **No exceptions**. This is one of my major pet peeves (can you tell?). If you do get to meet, keep it short – less than 15 minutes. Remember the selling artists have worked hard and been on their feet all day. They are probably very tired, and may be grumpy. It would be better if you meet at their studio at a better time. In other words, don't do anything to interfere with an artist doing business. They have spent a lot of time and money to be there.

Just like there are *serial killers*, there are also *serial artists*. They are regulars at shows and waste everyone's time. Don't become a *serial artist*, you will be found out and eventually ignored.

We were having one of our open house/studio sales one year; two artists brought their artwork into our studio show, laid it out on one of our tables, while the room was full of **our** clients. They wanted a critique of their work, wanted us to help them get into galleries, and kept interrupting us when we were with our clients, saying, *When you finish with them, I need you to see these new paintings.* Zap, that bridge went up in flames!

By interrupting you may stall a sale or totally blow it. If anyone enters a booth while you are talking, excuse yourself and GET OUT of the booth. Too many people clustered around can make buyers uncomfortable and they may leave without buying anything. Do not joke around in someone else's booth. You will drive away any potential sales you or your friend may have gained.

Don't drink alcohol during the show. People will notice your behavior and if you drink enough you will do something stupid, and you will smell of alcohol. Don't offend your clients before you even get started. Smoking is just as offensive. You smell, your clothes smell, and your breath is even worse.

Wear appropriate clothing. Some artists will dress up especially for the show. Wonderful, be creative. If you sell western work, dressing as a cowboy is ideal; you probably are one anyway. Some women have beautiful western outfits, which can be creative. My husband and I normally dress in

Safari clothes because we paint wildlife and collectors expect to see us this way. But we wear these at home anyway. Wear comfortable shoes. You will be standing for long hours. Torn shorts are appropriate for setting up and tearing your booth down, but not during show hours. Some shows are more casual than others, but the more professional you look the better you will be perceived by the buying public. Remember you can never be over dressed.

If a client asks your opinion of someone else's work, ALWAYS be positive about the work. You don't know to whom you are talking, or why they are asking. This is just common sense. You don't want someone knocking your artwork, so please, be respectful. Do not offer your unsolicited opinion of someone else's work unless you want to *die a slow and horrible death.* We have seen artists kill a sale for someone else without realizing what they have done. If you don't have something nice to say, KEEP YOUR MOUTH SHUT, especially around clients.

If you are showing at an event, leave your kids at home. There is no place for children running around a show bothering other artists and potential clients. Your job is to sell, not baby sit. It is definitely not the other artist's job to entertain your kids. Yes, your child is so cute; but not to everyone. Please leave them at home. Keep your pets at home as well; they don't belong in your booth.

Follow the Rules

If you are displaying at a show, follow the rules of the show. This is very important if you want to be asked to return in the future. Have all the required paperwork completed when they ask for it. Yes, I know, everyone hates paperwork. Hang your booth between the requested hours. Do not ask for special permission to come in late, especially if you are a new artist. Schedule your arrival the day before if necessary to insure you can set up

on time. Unload your car, and then park your car so other artists can set up. Be considerate of your neighbors when setting up your booth. Keep things out of the aisles; don't put your tools, chair, packing material, etc, in your neighbor's booth. Be considerate, and thoughtful. When you are finished if you see someone struggling, ask if they need your help.

Do not complain about your space, especially new artists. Emerging artists are generally placed at the bottom of the list for prime locations. Major shows want to include as many artists as possible, so the *newbe* will usually get the worst location. You will need to *prove* yourself (sell, sell $$$$) to receive the prime locations. This is part of the dues that a new artist has to pay. If you have a legitimate complaint discuss it in a professional manner, alone with the show organizers, when they have the time. Set up time is a madhouse and to put the organizer in a discussion, at that time, about your booth will not put you in good standing. There are exceptions, obviously. If your booth is under a dripping air conditioning unit, that is a valid problem because it could damage your artwork. If you are blocking a fire exit, that needs to be changed. Choose your battles wisely. Remember your reputation (especially if it is negative) will get around quickly. This may affect you for future shows, not just the current one. Organizers from different shows talk frequently, and you don't want to become known as the *problem child*, which may keep you out of any future shows. Rumors grow quickly and the result is usually much worse than the actual event. Better to be remembered as a professional considerate artist, than a bitchy, negative jerk.

One of the joys of working a show is talking to the other artists. Sometimes it is hard to remember why you are at the show because you are having so much fun talking to old friends. Remember that you and the other artists are there to SELL. Respect other artists when they have people in their booths; do not go into their space and interrupt or talk with them. You don't know if these are potential clients, old clients, or just friends. Please do not photograph other artists' work. Remember that the artwork is copyright protected. There are too many ways that the photograph of the artwork can end up in a country that doesn't recognize copyright law, on every mug and towel without the artist's permission, and without receiving a penny for the licensing. If you see someone photographing someone's artwork, ask him or her politely to stop, explaining that everything in the booth is copyright © protected, and that they should ask permission from the artist before photographing anything. If they ignore you, report them to the show security. We have seen people who are very sneaky about photographing artwork, using cell phones, or digital cameras hidden in jackets. There is no reason for someone to be photographing an artist's artwork, especially without his or her permission. Also you may innocently take a photo of someone's painting and later copy that painting. You could get sued. Please be respectful of the copyright laws.

If you want to get ahead as an artist take workshops from different artists, read books, watch videos. This is all part of your education. Take it seriously, if you want to be the best, and do whatever it takes to get the education in as many different ways as possible.

Attending Workshops

The best advice for anyone attending a workshop is: **arrive with an open mind, and a closed mouth**. The reason you signed up for the workshop is to *learn* what this instructor teaches. Other people in the class have paid a

lot of money to attend the workshop to *learn* from this instructor. We have taught numerous classes where someone in the class decides that they are a better artist, more famous (than the instructor is), have been teaching longer, are smarter, more creative, and think they should be teaching the class. If they feel like this, then they shouldn't be in class, they should be conducting one. When attending a class, there is so much information and techniques being discussed, there is always something an artist – no matter how accomplished, can take away from the class. There is a theory that attendees at a seminar, master class or workshop, only retain about 10% of what they hear. It becomes very confusing to students to have to listen to the instructor, and a know-it-all student. Most classes have someone attending who says things like *This is how I…; my way is faster; No, the way I….; I always…..; when I…; I can show everyone how I do this….* These people are very distracting, not to mention very annoying and should be ignored. Obviously you don't want to behave like this person nor should you pay attention to a class know-it-all.

Remember: **Winners do what losers won't.**

Review:

- Never burn your bridges.
- Never bring your portfolio into another artist's selling space.
- Serial Artists murder your time.
- Follow the Show Rules.
- Booth set up/breakdown consideration.
- Respect artist's selling time.
- Don't drink or smoke at a show.
- Wear appropriate professional clothing.
- Be positive about others artists' work.
- Leave the kids and pets at home.
- Visit other shows, all kinds.
- Please do not photograph another artist's work.
- Take lots of workshops.

Chapter 11

Defending yourself against stupidity
or... A funny thing happened to me on the way to the show

True Stories From Shows

Get ready! You will hear some strange things at art shows.

Here are real statements made to real artists. We did not make them up. If you are going to do shows you need a thick skin. Do not take anything personally that you hear at a show, except of course the good stuff.

Dennis Logsdon tells this story: "As a scratch board artist, I got used to unfamiliar remarks, but when I was doing a show in South Carolina a number of years ago I heard the best.

"It was the opening night Gala and a lovely woman, drink in hand, comes up to me and says: 'Does it bother you that there are 4 other scratch board artists in the show?'

"I looked at her and could not resist, I said: Yes, it does, as a matter of fact, I think every show should have one Watercolor artist, one Acrylic painter, one Oil painter and so on. It would make it easier for a nice client as yourself to choose work by the medium.

"I thought I was going to get her drink in my face. More than likely I deserved it."

Lee Cable – an internationally renowned artist who lives in Colorado drove for two days to a show in California. During the show a gentleman came up to Lee and asked to purchase Lee's largest painting, of an elk, for 45% off the price. Lee explained that he couldn't discount his paintings 45% because of all his costs involved in the show. The man was insistent and wanted 45% off. Lee then asked the man what was his profession. The man replied that he was a local Veterinarian. So Lee said:

"Tell you what, I will give you a 45% discount on my painting if you will drive from California to my home in Colorado, using your own money, stay in Colorado for a week, still using your money, and take care of my two horses for 45% off your normal vet bill."

The man said: "There is no way I am going to do that!" The man walked away, but still went to every artist in the show asking for a 45% discount.

My Painting is Done, Now What Do I Do? Simple Systems for Artists   By Suzie Seerey-Lester

During one show, a customer came up to my husband John, and asked: "Do you have your work in restaurants? You know, once you do, you really have made it."

Jokingly John replied: "Actually no, I don't, but I am in a lot of men's rooms."

The customer was happy with his response, and replied: "Well, don't worry you will make it one day."

Wes and Rachelle Siegrist are painters of miniatures, with the average size of their paintings about 2"x2". They shared this story:

"One completely sincere viewer was unable to believe that we actually painted our paintings that small. She was convinced that they had been painted larger and shrunk them. 'Do you put them in like…. an easy bake oven… to make them smaller?'"

My husband John's booth was set up so that next to each painting was a photograph of the painting, and a story about it. A wife said to her husband:

"These paintings are better than the photographs."

The husband explained they were photographs of the paintings. She said: "I don't care, the paintings are still better than the photographs."

John was the Featured Artist at the Southeastern Wildlife Expo (SEWE) in Charleston, S.C., one year. During the opening gala, while John was signing posters, (under a big banner that said *Meet Featured Artist John Seerey-Lester*); a gentleman came up to him and asked: "Do you have anything to do with this show?"

John replied: "Yes, can I help you with something?"

The man said: "Well, where is Carl Brenders?"

John politely said: "Carl will not be attending this year."

The man then asked insistently: "He has to be here, I have this, giving me a free book of his."

John took the paper and read it, telling the gentleman: "You mean Carl Rungius."

The man retorted gruffly: "Well, where is he then?"

"He's dead", John said.

The old man gasped in horror: "When did he die?"

"1928" John replied.

Julia Rogers, an internationally renowned artist, who contributed these two stories, had a beautiful painting of a sleeping leopard in a tree with its kill hanging over a branch on the opposite side of the tree.

The viewer asked:

"How would you get an antelope and a leopard to sleep in the same tree? I didn't know antelope could climb trees."

A couple came into her booth with a tape measure. Julia asked if they had any quest ions. The couple said: "No, we hate the artwork, but we like the frame and want it for our calendar."

The next story was contributed by TV/Radio Personality Jack Perkins, who is also a Poet and a Photographer.

A woman, looking at a display of his photographs, said to him: "Oh, I know where that is. That's at Fernandina Beach, isn't it?"

"Yes, ma'am."

"It's a beautiful place. Have you ever been there?", asked the woman.

"Can I get a discount after the show, if it doesn't sell?"

The response was: "Yes, if I can get all the restaurants, car rental companies, hotel and airlines I've used to get here, to give me a discount. I'll get back to you when I know."

When we asked a woman passing by "Are you enjoying the show?" Her response was: "No, but we had fun in Wal-Mart this morning."

Fran Sweet, an internationally known scratch board artist told us this story:

"A busload of mentally challenged people arrived at this particular art show. One of the group stopped at my booth and observed a large scratch board of an Indian Rhino. One person came over to me and asked: 'Is this for sale?'

"I replied: Yes, it is.

"When the man looked at the very expensive price tag, he cried out so loud everyone in the show heard: 'ARE YOU NUTS?'

"He then turned and ran out and got on the empty bus. I felt like I probably should have gotten on the bus myself. All I heard the rest of the show, from all the other artists was 'ARE YOU NUTS?'"

Linda Besse contributed this story: "A number of years ago, as I was painting at a show in Oklahoma, I watched an 8 year old girl walk into my booth and give a serious look around. Nodding her head in approval, she said my work was very nice. She added in a thoughtful and mature way:

'You know, if I can't be a dentist like I really want to be when I grow up, I will be an artist.'"

Kelly Dodge told us: "The very first show I ever participated in was during my last year of high school. Two students were chosen to participate in a *professional* art show called 10x10. This involved 10 artists, with 10 pieces of art each. The other eight artists were lovely little old ladies who did still life paintings of fruit and flowers. The other student and myself (late 1970's) were NOT painting fruit. During the *meet the artist day…* we were required to wear name tags. My hair, being very long, covered my tag. Standing not far from one of my best masterpieces, I overheard the comment in direct reference to my painting:

'It is too large for my outhouse.'

"Rather mortifying for a 16 year old who was hoping to make a career as an artist. I wonder if perhaps that comment had something to do with why I ended up working with children for 23 years before quitting 6 years ago to FINALLY pursue my once forgotten, but now very real, dream."

Customers looking at my husband John's original book, *Face to Face with Nature*, published in 1990, looked at the photo of a younger John on the jacket and asked John: "So do you miss him?"

Artist, Brendan Coudal told us these stories:
"After recently finishing two large game fish paintings (of which I was quite proud), I took them to be photographed. While waiting, I noticed that a gentleman (of very questionable character) was carefully looking them over. He caught my eye and said: 'Hey, these are pretty good… you should keep it up 'cause you're almost as good as that *'Kincade'* guy.'"

"During one of my rare plein air experiences, I had just set up all my stuff, then noticed a homeless man digging in a trash can, surrounded by raccoons. He saw me painting, came over (with a raccoon in tow, I recall) and asked what I was doing.

"I said: I am a wildlife artist.

"He asked, sarcastically: 'You can make a living at that?!?!'"

My Painting is Done, Now What Do I Do? Simple Systems for Artists   By Suzie Seerey-Lester

This was said to a gallery owner by a customer viewing an impressionistic painting: "At prices like these, you would think the artist could afford glasses."

"Glasses?" Asked the gallery owner.

"Everything is so fuzzy."

Pam Johnson Brickell, who once produced hand woven landscapes, tells of a couple looking at her time-consuming and very technical, art form, using corduroy and Theo Moorman weaving techniques, with lots of texture and color.

The husband said to the wife: "Now I know what happened to all them shag rugs from the 60's."

The following three stories come from Denis Leblanc:
People will say: "I can't draw a straight line."   Denis tells them:
"I can't either, I use a ruler."

"Where are you next week?"
 Denis says: "I may be dead next week, you need to purchase the painting now."

Denis told us: "I once had a guy ask me the price on my largest painting.

It was 29x50 inches, framed with museum glass and a two inch wide gold frame. I told him it was thirty-nine, ninety-five."

He said: "I'll take it."

"I proceeded to calculate the tax, which came to $199.75, and he just looked at me with this dumbfounded look and said: 'I thought you said $39.95.'"

Johanna Drummond told us this story: Her son, who was a Master Gunnery Sgt. Marines, used to help her at a show in Ft. Lauderdale. One time she left him in charge, while she took a break. An interested party came up and was looking very closely at one of her animal sculptures, and asked her son:

"Where did you get your eyes?"

My son replied: "From my Mom."

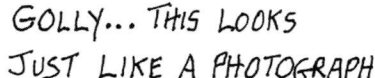

John Banovich said: "My favorite collector is the Whistling Gopher – he is the guy who walks up to a painting and says:
'Whets that go fer?'
"When you tell him, he just whistles and walks away."

A woman came into my booth and said "I like your painting so much, I am going to take a photograph of it, blow it up, and hang it on my wall."

A show visitor, incensed, viewing a large painting, a pale misty scene, the animal barely discernible: "How can you charge $40,000.00 for that painting, when there is hardly any paint on it?"

A customer asked me about giclée prints. Patiently, I explained the ink jet process only to hear him loudly reply:

"Oh, so they are fakes."

Kelly Dodge also sent this story:

"A woman walked past my art without appearing to look. Then turned around, came back, immediately picked up one of my rack card promotions, and told me, as she walked away, that it was going to make a lovely bookmark!"

I spent some time with three ladies discussing my bird paintings. Thinking I had a possible sale, I asked if they had any questions about the technique. One of the ladies piped up and said: "You should paint your eyelashes like mine."

I said: "I don't paint eyelashes on the birds."

The lady said: "No my eyelashes. Aren't they just beautiful?"

Toni Young shared these three stories:

Her late husband, Paco was painting in his booth at the end of a long, tiring show. The crowds had dwindled, and a little boy came into the booth. He wandered over to where Paco was painting to listen to the artist explain his techniques. The boy suddenly got a pained look on his face, turned white, then green, and proceeded to throw-up on Paco's palette.

Before the days of being politically correct, an old hated TV commercial: A little boy is seen painting a watercolor. The voice-over says: "This little boy was once called retarded … now he is an artist…."

A visitor walks into Paco's booth and asks: "Did you paint this?"
Paco replied: "Why, Yes, I did."
"Then who painted all the rest of them?"

Tom Krause, is a Nationally known marine artist, specializing in Florida fish and mammals. Here are some of the comments he has heard:

"Isn't it hard to get your paints to dry, when you paint underwater?"

"How do you get the fish to stop swimming?"

"I like the frame that you have on this painting."
Tom replies: "Well, thank you."
"I just bought this great painting from a someone else here at the show, will you make me that frame for the painting?"

Finally, the worst comment to hear. . . "it doesn't really matter what the subject is as long as it matches the couch."

Joking apart, the above stories are a sample of the types of comments you will receive at shows. The important thing is how you handle the comments, without insulting potential clients and appearing like a smart ass, which will offend some people. There is a fine line between responding humorously and being insulting. Bare in mind, many of these comments and the responses by the artists have come at the end of a long and sometimes frustrating show. Nerves are frayed from a succession of seemingly stupid insulting comments the artists have heard over and over. Your reaction will also be directly related to how many pieces you sell. If you sell-out, then every one of these stories is a *laugh-a-minute*. If you have not done well, then they will haunt you forever. Always show respect to the visitors at shows. These are potential clients and if you handle them properly, they may turn into buyers.

Chapter 12

Recommended Resource List

Certificates
- **Regal Mills** Premium Certificates
8½x11 heavyweight paper
Any Office Supply/Stationery Store

Clear Print Sleeves
- **Crystal Clear Bags**
  - *West coast:*
  4949 Windplay Drive #100
  El Dorado Hills, CA 95762
  1800 233 2630
  - *East coast:*
  4872 Highway 64 East
  PO Box 307
  Selmer, TN 38375
  1800 328 1847
  www.clearbags.com

Copyright ©
- **US Copyright Office**
101 Independence Ave S.E.
Washington, D.C. 20559-6000
www.copyright.gov

- **Intellectual Property Specialist**
Mr. Joshua Kaufman
The Venable Group
1201 New York Avenue, NW,
Suite 1000,
Washington, DC 20005
(202) 344-8538
jjkaufman@venable.com

Easels
- **Hughes Easels**
1 800-485-6081
www.hugheseasels.com

Framing

- **JFM Enterprises** (gold frames)
4476 Park Drive
Norcross, GA 30093
1 800-462-3449

- **LaTourette** (wood frames)
1 888-523-7263
www.LaFrame.com

- **Graphik Dimensions, Ltd**
2103 Brentwood Street
High Point, NC 27263
1 800-221-0262
www.pictureframes.com

- **Dominus Frames**
1 480-449-1000
www.dominusframes.com

- **Tara Picture Frames**
1 800-788-9969
www.tarapf.com

- **Florida Frames**
1 800-878-3946
www.floridaframes.com

- **Artful Picture Frames**
1 800-840-4738
www.artfulpictureframes.com

- **Picture Framing Point Driver**
(Logan Picture Framing System Model F500-1)
Available at Jerry's, or any art supply company

- **Phillips Flat Sheet Metal Screws**
Zinc Screws 8 x ½
Any Hardware Store

- **Picture Wire**
4x25 Feet 40 lb
Any Hardware Store and some Art Supply Stores/Catalogs

- **Paper Backing for Frames**
Any Office Supply/Stationary Store

- **Name Plates**
Allysons
21 A Cote Drive,
Epping, NH 03042
www.titleplates.com

- **D-Rings** – Large or Medium
Any Hardware Store and some Art Supply Stores/Catalogs

- **Electric Screwdriver** (drill)
Any Hardware Store

Labels

- **Avery Labels Address Labels**
#8160, 8163, 8164
Any Office Supply/Stationary Store

Listing of Art Shows

- **Howard Alan Events. Ltd**
9695 West Broward Blvd
Plantation, FL 33324
1 954-472-3755
www.artfestival.com

■ **Lake Mary** –
Heathrow Festival of the Arts
PO Box 952125
Lake Mary, Fl 32795
1 407-444-0484
www.lakemaryheathrowarts.com

■ **Sunset Boulevard Promotions**
1959 Rolling Green Circle
Sarasota, FL 34240
www.sunsetboulevardpromotions.com

Photos/Slides & Transparencies
■ **DPI Art Services**
2639 Minnehaha Avenue
Minneapolis, MN 55406
1 888-721-3259
www.dpiartservices.com

Plein Air Equipment
■ **Open Box M**
1 800-473-8090

Shipping
■ **Flat Cardboard Sheets**
Any Art Supply or Box Company

■ **Rolls of Plastic Sheeting**
Any Hardware Store

■ **Federal Express**
1 800-463-3339
www.fedex.com

■ **UPS**
1 800-742-5877
www.ups.com

■ **Shipping Crates** *Local Handyman*

■ **Strongboxes**
110 Elizabeth Street
PO Box 220
Tupelo, MS 38802
1 800-445-2580
sales@airfloatsystems.com

■ **Picture Shipper ™**
1 800-214-7115
www.packagedepot.com/PicShip.htm

■ **Cardboard Boxes**
Any Shipping/Storage/Box company

Show Tents
■ **CraftHut Tents**
Flourish Company
3640 Highway 23
St. Paul, AR 72760
1 800-678-8677
www.flourish.com

Show Panels
■ **Mesh Panel Display Walls**
Flourish Company
3640 Highway 23
St. Paul, AR 72760
1 800-678-8677
www.flourish.com

Pro Panels MD Enterprises
9017 Diplomacy Row
Dallas, TX 75247
1 800-525-4159

www.propanels.com

■ **Graphic Display Systems**
308 South First Street
Lebanon, PA 17042
1 800-848-3020
www.graphicdisplaysystems.com

Slides
■ **DPI Art Services**
2639 Minnehaha Avenue
Minneapolis, MN 55406
1 888-721-3259
www.dpiartservices.com

■ **Colorslide.com**
1 614-866-4376
www.colorslide.com

■ **Gammatech.com**
www.gammatech.com

Slide Labels
■ **Image Innovations Inc.**
Slide Pro Labels LL-SR
1 800-345-4118

Software
■ **Microsoft Word**
Any Computer Retailer
www.microsoft.com

■ **Microsoft Excel**
Any Computer Retailer
www.microsoft.com

■ **Working Artist Software**
7700 Earling St NE
Olympia, WA 98506
1 800-897-3758.
info@workingartist.com
www.workingartist.com

■ **QuickBooks**
www.quickbooks.intuit.com

■ **Hewlett-Packard Free Software**
HP Marketing Assistant *Lite*
www.hp.com

Varnish
■ **Varnish, Acrylic**
Krylon Crystal Clear
Any Art Supply Store/Catalog

■ **Varnish, Oil**
Damar Retouch Varnish
Any Art Supply Store/Catalog

■ **Varnish**
Liquin
Any Art Supply Store/Catalog

WC Book
■ **Accounting Book** – 8 Columns

■ **Microsoft Excel**
Any Computer Retailer
www.microsoft.com

Image Index

Documents

Bill of Sale   90
Booth Plan   106
Care & Handling of Acrylic   93
Care & Handling of Oil   94
Certificate of Original Art   92
Cert. of Original Art w/ photo   91
Commercial Invoice   101
Consignment Agreement   78
Copyright Label   21
Inventory of Originals   26
Newsletter   73
Notice Labels   22
Original Information Sheet   16
Painting Paragraph   71
Painting Paragraph/foam core   119
Painting Label   20
Photographer Release Letter   30
Price Tag   118
Recommended Retail Price (framed)   87
Show Check List   124, 125
Show Inventory List   104
Sold Inventory List   27
VIP Program   72
Where Have They Been   28
Work Completed Book   18
Work Completed Book by Alpha   19
Working Price Sheet (unframed)   85

Framing

"D" Ring attached to paper back   56
"D" Ring with wire   50
"D" Ring with both sides attached   57
Back of Paintings with 3 labels   48
Documents on back of frame   58
Double sided tape   54
Mirror Clip on canvas   47
Mirror Clip on masonite   47
Name Plate   59
Paper back being secured   55
Paper back being trimmed   55
Paper back completed   56
Paper back being measured   54
Point Driver securing painting   48
Points securing painting   49
Presentation folder w/ documents   58
Labeled paper back of frame   59
Sleeve for back of frame   57
Wire for back of painting   49

Photographing Your Artwork

Properly photographing painting   **38**
Photo album   **70**
Poor photos of paintings   **32-37**
Properly Photographed Painting   **38**
Slide Binder   **41**
Silver Tape being applied to slide   **40**
Silver Tape on slide complete   **40**
Slide properly labeled   **42**
Slides in slide sheet   **41**
Transparency on light box   **43**

Shows

Booth Set up, paintings hung   **107**
Box System in garden cart   **105**
John in his booth   **108**
Outdoor show with tent   **115**
Outdoor show tent set up   **115**
Painting in booth   **107**
Painting paragraph next to painting   **119**
Suzie & Florida Panther in booth   **109**
Suzie in her Booth   **108**

Shipping

Crate with photo inside lid   **97**
Picture shipper   **99**
Tie wrap on Picture Shipper   **99**
Picture shipper step one   **98**

Key Points Index

Auctions **126, 127**
Bad Photographs **32, 33, 34, 35, 36, 37**
Bill of Sale **90, 91**
Biography **66, 95**
Booth Plan **105, 106**
Booth Set Up **106, 109**
Booth, leaving **120**
Box System **104**
Burning Bridges **129**
Business Name & License **65, 66**
Care and Handling **92, 93, 94**
Certificate of Original Artwork **92**
Clients, Dealing Direct **79, 80, 81**
Commercial Invoice **100, 101**
Commissions **68, 69**
Consignment Agreement **77, 78, 79, 96**
Copyright **62, 63, 64, 79**
Copyright Label **21**
Crates **97**
Follow the rules **133, 134**
Frame Costs **86**
Frame, Nameplate **60**
Frames, Custom **51, 52**
Frames, Ordering **52**
Frames, Pricing **51**
Framing **50**
Framing under glass **52, 53**

Inventory of Originals **25, 26**
Label the Painting **20**
Licensing **64**
Logo **66**
Mentor **84, 85**
Newsletter **73, 74**
Notice Label **22**
Original Information Sheet **15, 16, 62**
Packaging **97**
Painting Paragraph **71, 72**
Photo Album **70**
Photograph, The Proper Way **38**
Photographing Art
 30, 31, 32, 33, 34, 35, 36, 37, 39
Photographing Art, Slides
 39, 40, 41, 42
Photographing Art, Transparency **43**
Photography, Professional **29**
Price Cards **118**
Price Tags **118**
Pricing **83, 85**
Pricing by Inch **86**
Procedures Manual **61**
Recommended Retail Price **86, 87**
Sales **120, 121, 122, 123**
Sales, Open Studio **74, 75**
Scrapbook **69, 70**

Shipping Internationally **100**
Shipping to a Client **89**
Show breakdown **126**
Show Check List **123, 124, 125**
Show clothing **131, 132**
Show Inventory List **103, 104**
Show, kids, pets **132**
Shows, true stories **137-150**
Software **70, 71**
Sold Inventory **26, 27**
Specialized Boxes **98, 99**
Tents **114, 115, 116, 117, 118**

Thank You Note **95**
Using a Point Driver Gun **47, 48, 49**
Varnishing Acrylic Paintings **45**
Varnishing Oil Paintings **46**
VIP Program **72, 73**
WC Book (Work Completed)
    17, 18, 19
Website **67, 68**
Where Have They Been **27, 28**
Workshops, attending **134, 135**

Master Series of DVDs by John Seerey-Lester
There are 24 different DVD's in this series...
12 in oil & 12 in acrylic.

- Each DVD in the series is approximately 90 minutes long.
- You can choose to watch John paint in either oil or acrylic.
- Each DVD shows a different painting technique.
- You as the artist can decide the area in which you would like instruction.

DVD's Available

Master Series
by John Seerey-Lester
- **Complete Set of 24 DVD's**
  $995.00 + S&H
  (covering both oil and acrylic)
- **Set of 12 DVD $595.00** + S&H
  (covering either oil or acrylic)
- **Individual: $59.00 ea** + S&H
  (covering either oil or acrylic)

Vol. I	Painting Fur
Vol. II	Painting Animals
Vol. III	Painting Birds
Vol. IV	Painting in the Field
Vol. V	Painting Snow
Vol. VI	Painting Water
Vol. VII	Painting Elements
Vol. VIII	Painting Landscapes
Vol. IX	Painting Action
Vol. X	Painting Skies
Vol. XI	Composition & Light
Vol. XII	Creating Atmosphere

On the Easel Series of DVD's by John Seerey-Lester
New Series of 90 minute DVD's now Available!

Each DVD shows John painting one complete painting from start to finish. John explains his thought process as you watch him paint. He starts the painting in front of your eyes, changes it, moves things around, as you watch him in the step by step process of designing, creating, changing, using different techniques, and finally the completed painting comes to life. His light-hearted commentary during this painting is both entertaining and informative.

On The Easel by John Seerey-Lester
Sold in DVD format only / Each DVD is $59.00, + S&H

Polar Impact - Oil
Sonora Majesty - Oil
Campfire Shadows - Acrylic

Wildscape Series of DVD's by John Seerey-Lester
Look out for the new Wildscape DVD series, which takes you from the wild to the completed painting in the studio.

Wildscape by John Seerey-Lester
Lost - Acrylic (Sold in DVD format only)

To Order John Seerey-Lester DVD's:
Phone: 941-966-2163 or 941-484-6164
Email: **seereylester@msn.com**   Website: **www.seerey-lester.com**

Comments from Suzie;

Thank you for purchasing **"My Painting Is Done, Now What Do I Do?**

Your feedback on the book is important to me and I want to hear from you. Please let me know what you liked about the book, what you feel should be included in the reprinting of the book, or what should be left out.

If you have systems that you have used over the years that work, let me know about them as well. Many artists will have funny stories about their experiences as they are working or selling, so please include them and let me know that it is ok to publish the stories.

We would also like to include you in our mailing list for future books, DVD's newsletters, and projects in which you may be interested. **Please give us your name, address, phone number and e-mail address.**

Please send your comments to:
Suzie Seerey-Lester
Mermaid Press, LLC
"Treetops"
208 Shoreland Drive
Osprey, Florida 34229

Email: **seereylester@msn.com**
Website: **www.seerey-lester.com**